W9-CFJ-988

PRAISE FOR OTHER WORKS BY KEN CAREY

Flat Rock Journal

"For those interested in the spiritual aspects of nature, this book is a real find. Carey's modesty, kindness, and intelligence emanate . . . from every page."

—*Los Angeles T*

"Humorous, warm, insightful, and a delight to read."
—*Library Journal*

"A model of moss-velvet nature writing, quite possibl classic."

—*Kirku*

Return of the Bird Tribes

"A stunning, shimmering, joyful experience. . . . "
—Dr. Wayne Dyer, author of *Your Er*

The Starseed Transmissions

"At once lyrical and hearty, offering a substa nature of the spiritual and evolutionary pur
—Jean Houston, Ph.D., author of *7*

THE THIRD MILLENNIUM

ALSO BY KEN CAREY

The Starseed Transmissions

Vision

Return of the Bird Tribes

Flat Rock Journal

THE THIRD MILLENNIUM

LIVING IN THE
POSTHISTORIC WORLD

Ken Carey

HarperSanFrancisco
A Division of HarperCollins*Publishers*

HarperSanFrancisco and the author, in association with The Basic Foundation, a not-for-profit organization whose primary mission is reforestation, will facilitate the planting of two trees for every one tree used in the manufacture of this book.

Workshops and Seminars

For information on workshops and seminars by Ken Carey, write:

Starseed Seminars
Star Route, Box 70
Mountain View, Missouri 65548

THE THIRD MILLENNIUM: *Living in the Posthistoric World.* Copyright © 1991 by Ken Carey. Foreword copyright © 1995 by Marianne Williamson. All rights reserved. Printed in the United States of America. No part of this book may be used or reproduced in any manner whatsoever without written permission, except in the case of brief quotations embodied in critical articles and reviews. For information, address HarperCollins Publishers, 10 East 53rd Street, New York, NY 10022.

ORIGINALLY PUBLISHED AS STARSEED, THE THIRD MILLENNIUM.

Library of Congress Cataloging-in-Publication Data
Carey, Ken.
[Starseed, the third millennium]
The third millennium : living in the posthistoric world / Ken Carey.
p. cm.
Previously published as: Starseed, the third millennium. c1991.
ISBN 0–06–251244–7
1. New Age movement. 2. Channeling (Spiritualism) I. Title.
[BP605.N48C384 1995]
133.9'3—dc20
94-39494
CIP

95 96 97 98 99 RRD(H) 10 9 8 7 6 5 4 3 2 1

This edition is printed on acid-free paper that meets the American National Standards Institute Z39.48 Standard.

Contents

Contents

Foreword

Authors are often asked, "And what do *you* read?" When I am asked which books are on my bedside table, I always say Ken Carey's *The Third Millennium* because it remains there permanently.

I read it, ponder it, underline parts in yellow, tell other people to read it and buy copies for my friends. At one point, I even called the publisher to put in my two cents worth on how the book should be published. I couldn't imagine that this book wasn't yet known by almost everyone in the world. It has seemed obvious to me, from the first time I read Carey's writing, that if ever there was a treasure in our midst, it's this gentle man in Missouri who is so clearly plugged in to the sun and the moon and the stars in the sky.

What is it about Ken Carey and *The Third Millennium* that I think is so great? First, Carey is a master poet; his language is some of the most beautiful I have ever read. But more important, it is his *information* that is so outrageous. Somehow, somewhere, he was given the keys to our future, and he generously and skillfully passes the secrets on to the rest of us.

I'm fascinated by anything millennial. What's going to happen, how we're going to manage, what it's going to look like, who we'll be—these are subjects that magnetize my attention. Magazine articles, books, lectures, whatever—I'll read or I'll listen. But what Ken Carey writes about the historical chapter ahead and our part in it if we choose is so magical and profound that this book is, for me, a kind of Millennial Bible.

I have referred to it many times and I will refer to it many times again.

We are living at a very exciting moment in time. Transformational information is to the nineties what rock 'n' roll was to the sixties. And what made rock 'n' roll so exciting then was not one particular group or individual: what made it so awesome was the whole array of genius.

Today, there is an array of spiritual, metaphysical wisdom among us. Ken Carey is one of the great living teachers, one of the stars that make the dark sky bearable. Read him and you'll have hope. He sheds light and faith and absolute conviction that not only is the future nothing any of us have to fear, but that indeed, the best for humanity is still to come. Ken Carey is clearly a signpost. How wonderful that *The Third Millennium* is here.

Marianne Williamson

Preface

It was December 27. I was in bed with a fever, yet I felt more elated than ill. Something about the consciousness I was swimming in, living, being in, seemed strangely familiar, as if my vision were coming into focus after a lifetime of double images. Without the calm reasoning guidance of the voice I heard speaking to me, I am not sure I would have made it through this stage. But someone—or something—was helping me along, identifying itself as a part of me that I had forgotten, an eternal part.

"I am a spirit being in the eternal fields of light," it said. "I am you as you remain beyond material illusion, as you were, will be, and are now, before and after the spell of matter."

My handwriting being quite illegible, my only method of recording anything of the amazing stream of consciousness I had somehow stumbled upon was to type what I could of it on an old Royal portable typewriter that my brother-in-law found sitting on the curbside one day as he made his rounds as a garbage collector in Darien, Connecticut. But it was a strange sort of communication, unsettling at first.

I found myself experiencing a consciousness radically different from anything I had ever before encountered. And it was too close for comfort. I felt as if something enormous were looking through my eyes, seeing the same room I saw every day but interpreting it so differently—mathematically, it seemed—that I hardly recognized even the most familiar of my daily objects. The thoughts, the ideas, the scope of the images—I was not used to thinking in such terms. I was unprepared, and not always able to follow. I balked in outright disbelief when the voice first suggested that this was some kind of extraterrestrial intelligence I was encountering—an explanation that even now I do not accept without qualification. But despite the fact that my mind frequently lagged behind, on an emotional level my heart and soul were experiencing a blissful, almost sexual, feeling of fulfillment.

I felt a peace that I could not account for, a sense of well-being deeper than I had ever known. When I understood what was being said, it was so wonderful that I felt like a child on Christmas morning. In a strange way it was almost as if I were remembering things rather than being told them. It was all I could do to keep my fingers in the vicinity of the ancient machine that, thanks to a generous dose of WD-40, was continuously tapping out some partial account of the thoughts that were rippling wavelike through my awareness. Several times I forgot to put wood in the stove until my numb feet reminded me of the winter creeping in under the door.

When this experience continued into a second day, I told my wife, Sherry, that although I did not understand what was going on, I felt a need to follow through with it and see where it was leading. I asked her to make sure that I was not disturbed for the next few days. "If our friends or neighbors come over," I said, "ask them to come back another time. I need to be isolated until this process, whatever it is, is complete."

That night, six inches of wet snow blanketed the forest around our home.

By morning all the younger pine trees along both sides of the one-mile dirt road that ends in our yard had bent over under the snow's weight. There must have been a hundred of them bowing protectively across the road when I looked out the window the next morning.

Since we had no electricity, television, or radio in those days, the snow-laden trees effectively cut off all access to the outside world—and they remained that way until the transmissions were complete.

The fact that I had not previously known how to type must have been overlooked in the swirl of heightened consciousness, for when I awoke on the morning of January 6, 1979, there were 350 double-spaced typewritten pages stacked upon my desk—and my life had forever and irreversibly changed.

Throughout those eleven days, as I was typing the notes that would later be published as *The Starseed Transmissions,* I was told again and again by the entities who were blending with me that a much stronger surge of *telepathic awareness* was to be pulsed into the collective field of human consciousness between the years 1987 and 1989. It was emphasized that this would be far more powerful than the thought signals I was then receiving.

This prediction turned out to be as precise as if it had been drawn from a moon calendar or a table of the tides. Ten years later, during the same period, telepathic messages began coming in, like subtle music in the background of my thought at first, then stronger, and finally with such power that I decided to stop everything and begin recording them. Since what I had captured on paper in the earlier *Starseed Transmissions* was such a small percentage of the overall information flow I had received, I had resolved by this time to be better prepared.

By speaking aloud into a tape recorder while receiving this present material, I was able to bypass the manual distractions of the typewriter and translate much more of the awareness into the spoken word. Afterward, precise word-for-word transcription on a word processor brought into printed form a far more detailed and substantive account of the consciousness flow than had been possible ten years earlier. Admittedly, my process was not perfect. I still had to stop now and then to put a log in the stove or adjust the window, but my distractions were kept to a minimum, and I am very happy with the result, which I am pleased to share with you in the form of this book.

It was written during a season of global miracles. No *local* snow storm this time. In the 1970s I needed the validation of that dramatically timed snow cover to remind me that I lived in an intelligent and benevolent universe. Now I wonder how I could have ever forgotten.

But what exactly is this process?

I have yet to find a single word that adequately describes it.

After a decade of hearing the term *channeling* bantered about, I am convinced that it does not apply to the process through which I access this information. (I know many people who regularly tap into this awareness and I expect they would agree.) There is no trance involved in my reception of these thoughts, no loss of consciousness, no voice change or foreign accent. *I* am fully present throughout the experience. During the months that followed the recording of those first *Starseed Transmissions*, I began to realize that accessing higher-frequency awareness is actually an organic process, a natural ability with which every child is born. I have since devoted several years to studying preschool children, and though my work is not scientific and far from conclusive, I am personally convinced that this inborn ability usually atrophies with the acquisition of language.

As children develop language skills, they acquire the prevalent cultural belief that *if it cannot be put into words, it is not real*, or at least has no value or relevance. Since higher-frequency thought, or what is sometimes called *metapersonal* thought, is entirely nonverbal, as children are inculcated with cultural values they gradually stop noticing that they are living in a veritable ocean of nonverbal awareness. Can you imagine something so prevalent that it is entirely forgotten? As in the joke in which the student fish asks the philosopher fish, "What is this *ocean* you keep talking about?"

But perhaps *atrophy* is too strong a word. The ability to access higher-frequency thought can, of course, be reactivated. In a few cases, like my own, that reactivation occurs by accident, but—as thousands of letters bundled in our storeroom attest—it can also be reactivated intentionally.

The central chapters of this book take a closer look at this. They are sufficiently detailed to provide those interested with the basic tools of understanding required to regain their spirit-world sensitivity. Once you know what to look for, it is not difficult. It is essentially a matter of *listening*, of sensing, of feeling more fully, of opening to frequencies of thought that are normally filtered out of awareness.

I experience it as a process of relaxing into a more generalized and generous definition of self, a sort of spreading out, as it were, into a larger field of awareness. That larger field of awareness includes my center of human individuality, but it includes other centers of individuality as well. I experience these as aspects of myself—not my human self, but that deeper *eternal self* that all creatures share.

Call the process what you will—channeling, creative thinking, visioning, or simply perceiving more fully—it has opened me up to ways of considering reality that I am certain would not otherwise have occurred to me. In practical realms such as relationships, child rearing, gardening, and finance, it has introduced ingenious perspectives and creative interpretations that have proven themselves again and again. I sometimes wonder how different the course of my life might have been had I learned to listen earlier to these inner frequencies. So much has changed since those eleven magical winter days.

When I recorded the original *Starseed Transmissions*, I was a rural carpenter who had been supporting a family for the past six years on an income of less than one-third of what was then officially defined as the U.S. poverty level. Our garden and milk cow ensured that was always had plenty of wholesome food, and though Sherry and I put in long hours, we were both relatively content. I enjoyed my work and anticipated a future along similar lines.

Today my life is so different, so radically altered, that at times I flash back to those pre-Starseed days and recall them with the black-and-white associations usually reserved for old photographs. Even now I can hardly explain the change. It was like suddenly poking my head up through the clouds to see the sunlight for the first time, or discovering a vast, new world beyond the cultural stage props that had previously defined my reality.

Something happens to you when you begin to think about this planet as a single living organism. And when you begin to *live in that awareness,* nothing is ever again quite the same. Nothing *can be* the same after that. Nations began to look like people to me, like familiar friends. The distinctions between religion, biology, and politics began to blur. I began to wonder why I had always assumed that *human thought* was the only kind of thought—as if nature would be content with a single species of flower, or just one kind of tree.

Whether or not you accept my own premise that the current of consciousness recorded in the following chapters is of angelic or extraterrestrial origin should in no way affect your experience of this book. The perspectives presented here are designed to stimulate your own processes of thought and understanding. Their purpose is catalytic—to trigger memory and awaken higher-dimensional sensitivity. I recommend taking your time before drawing too many conclusions about this material. Many of my own early assumptions proved invalid as I became more immersed in *the consciousness behind the words.*

We take identity too seriously. It isn't a fixed commodity like a table or a chair. Healthy individuality is a fluid, flowing focus of awareness, adjusting naturally to the ever-changing contours of time. It knows itself as one of many *eyes of eternity,* coalescing in an infinite sea of shared being. Individuals come and go like the waves of the sea, but at their core each one is first and foremost *the sea*, and only secondly the wave. Cultural programming prevents us from realizing this. It discourages true individuality. There have been a few genuine individuals during historical times, but not many, and those, of course, were individual because they knew the eternal Being at their core.

Some of the views and principles presented here may be new to you, others more familiar. But experiment with them. Apply them. See if they work. Let your own experience determine their degree of relevance. None of them are presented as absolute statements of truth. Truth does not lend itself to absolutes, linguistic or otherwise. The world has seen enough dogmatism. This book is about spirit. It is written for people of spirit.

If these words help even just a few of us to become more aware, they will have served their purpose.

Ken Carey
Greenwood Forest, Missouri

*Reading out of doors
in a quiet natural setting,
perhaps under a tree,
alongside a brook,
or near the seashore,
will greatly enhance
your experience
of what follows . . .*

1

The Boundaries of Time

The last of our communications to take place on conceptual levels will be sent during the years 1987 and 1989. This will be a truly momentous time, a time when the first contractions of (planetary) birth are unmistakable.

—THE STARSEED TRANSMISSIONS, DECEMBER 31, 1978

In these pages, we address you in a succession of different modes to ensure every possibility of your understanding and to maximize your opportunities to catch these thought currents and ride them beyond mere words to remembrance of your eternal nature and your root purpose for currently being incarnate on earth in human form. Therefore, we speak to you at times as if you were still sleeping beneath the blankets of material plane illusion. For in fact, this is the present state of the human majority.

At other times we speak to you as if you yourself were the One who is awakening into the collective field of human consciousness. This is valid; it is how you will soon understand the "I" behind your outer roles and images of self. To the extent that you oscillate back and forth, at times

experiencing moments of lucidity and oneness with the unified field of awareness, and at times lapsing back into the
familiar thought patterns of the prevailing cultural myth-
ology, you will find both forms of address of equal value.

Allow your understanding of who you are to relax as
you move through these pages. The historical limitations in
which you have defined yourself are no longer valid; indeed,
they never were.

Your eternal nature is much greater than the conceptions of time in which you have kept it defined. Release all
that you are from the prison of your self-concepts, that we
might become one in your understanding as we have always
been one in reality. Allow present-moment awareness to
flow freely among your thoughts.

You have created your body as a terrestrial terminal for
the habitation of eternal awareness. You have designed eyes
to interpret a portion of your energy spectrum and ears to
interpret another. You have created five senses to have a
window into these times upon this world, that, biologically
clothed, you might better monitor and interact with these
physical dimensions. You can no longer afford to sleep in the
illusions of this culture, allowing the wonders of sensory
input to confuse your sense of being with the information
you receive. The times you live in require the activation of
the full range of your eternal capacities. They call now—as
we do—for your incarnation.

When you define yourself without regard to your source
in the Eternal Presence out of which this universe unfolds,
when you continue to play out variations of the historical
theme, which keep your eternal spirit at arm's length by
imagining absolute "others" in the world around you, the
illusions of the material realm weigh heavily upon your consciousness. Forces that were intended only to hold energy
firmly within atomic structure bind and limit your perception. Your outlook becomes sober; your vision blurs beneath
the emotional mists of excessive subjectivity.

As gravity draws objects to fall, so too does it draw the thoughts of those who define themselves without reference to the Source. And with their thoughts, their identities fall as well, back into matter, again and again. So it was said to the first egos who began to think of themselves in this fictitious way, "In dust you have conceived yourselves and to dust you will return." For all thought is dust in the minds of those who deny the reality that seeks birth in the manger of human form.

When you define yourselves in isolation, your senses deceive and blind. They lock you into a fractional perception of the universe in which you live. Cultural illusions become your reality, filtering and misinterpreting everything you perceive. Like murky glass, they intervene between you and your understanding of self and world. They cut off awareness of your eternal origin and leave you with an inadequate sense of self.

In the historical condition human beings undertake the arduous task of self-definition. To receive assistance in this monumental work, they accept the help of others in their sleeping society and in time come to think of themselves as a loose assortment of images and illusions, often contradictory, always uninspired. The vibrancy of their eternal presence is blocked by ancestral preconceptions that have not known fundamental change since their forebears huddled in the hollows of the ancient hills.

Those who later in life realize the limitations of this "poor self-image" often seek to improve their image of self. Yet in undertaking a task that in the natural order belongs solely to the life force itself, they succeed only, if they succeed at all, in remodeling their prisons; they may replace bars of iron with bars of brass, but the prison remains. Within it their awareness stays limited and confined.

There is but the finest veil between you and a full-dimensional perception of reality, the filmiest of screens between you and your eternal self. You require no elaborate technique or ritual to release this veil. You need only open to the organic current of awareness that in every moment flows to you from the source of all life.

When you accept the understanding that accompanies *the awareness of your life force,* you are defined no longer in the static images of yesterday's experience but in active universal participation. You know yourself as an agent of the continuing creation that is the great purpose and the great joy of these material realms.

Though opening to *life force awareness* is as easy as relaxation, deliberation is needed to sustain such openness in a society where subconscious patterns continuously beckon you back into their familiar habits. Yet if your love for reality is sufficiently strong, such deliberation is not difficult. Nothing can stop those whose hearts burn with genuine passion for the truth. And the truth you will discover is worth your passion. For the awareness that accompanies the current of your life is an eternal awareness. It is the awareness of your spirit.

The self-understanding you receive in the experience of your eternal spirit is living, fluid, organic.

You are the creator of all you survey. You know your body as a system of exquisite biological circuitry designed to project your vision into this material world and bring your awareness into sharp and immediate environmental focus. You know yourself as an expression of universal Being, as a cell in the terrestrial body of the One whose consciousness is now awakening in the human family, a consciousness that is ultimately, and beautifully, your own.

One Being is the source of all creatures. The life of that Being shines through the multiple prisms of diverse worlds, refracting, reflecting, becoming the many, yet remaining ever one in essence, like the colors of a spectrum or the cells of a body.

The distinction between you and this Being is not absolute but organic, like the distinction between leaves on a tree or the distinction between notes that contribute to the harmonies of a song. Behind your individuality, beneath your cultural images of self, *that Being is who you are.* We bring you these transmissions that you might come to live once again as we do, in full consciousness of your source.

All that stands between you and awareness of the Being at the source of life can be released as easily as a sigh. Even now, you are but a breath away from the subtle perceptual shift that allows your identity to be transformed from solitary individual to the source of every individual, from the object of attention to the very flow of attention itself, from the contents of consciousness to the awareness that brings all content to light. When you know yourself in this way, you recognize the others of your kind. You perceive us. We communicate. As our communication flows into communion, you recognize yourself in us. You awaken to awareness of our common source.

We are beings consciously inhabiting the universal Presence. In the fields of space and time we individualize qualities of the same Being we share with you, even as you have also individualized other qualities of that Being. Though not all of us have chosen, as you have chosen, to dress in human form, still, we are your family within time, your sisters, your brothers. Beyond time, we are one.

We are a race of voyagers, spirit beings in the eternal fields of light; yet we are you yourselves as you would have been had you not succumbed to the spell of matter.

We are you as you remain beyond material illusion, addressing in these pages a sleeping part of ourselves that you might awaken and know this awareness as your own. We would shine the light upon the reality of your presence from behind you, from above you, from beneath you, that at last you might recognize that light within you and awaken.

There is only one who sleeps, though that one sleeps beneath five billion varying blankets of human illusion. And there is but one who awakens, and awakening, wears the blankets of former illusion as transformed robes of luminous biology.

There is no word in this language that conveys the meaning of *I, you,* and *we* simultaneously. Yet it is in this understanding that these transmissions originate, and it is to this understanding that they lead. You are on both sides of this communication, giving and receiving, both forming these thoughts and being informed.

We know within us a center of being that is itself beyond temporal creations. Centered in eternal identity, we are free to travel throughout the realms of past and future. Yet those among us who take on material form always do so in linear time. This is not a limitation; it is the mechanism of creation's frame. No artist would set out to paint a boundless canvas that stretched infinitely into all directions. So it is that we establish the parameters of the manifest worlds, framing each space in the boundaries of time.

We have long known that a turning point would come in the unfoldment of this universal art, after which human beings would be our primary means of future creation, as well as the organ of awareness through whom we would interpret and enjoy the material plane. That time is now. We invite you to leave behind your historical impressions of the human experience that you might rise to your natural level of consciousness.

Your human body has been designed to allow your self-awareness to ride upon the crest of creation's wave—*at that precise breaking point where the one eternal wave splashes into the many and into their linear worlds of time.* As a representative projection of eternity, a nerve ending of God-in-matter, you remain conscious of eternal unity even while experiencing yourself as part of diversity's material fabric.

To be the One and simultaneously the many—this is your calling, your purpose, the ultimate destiny of your kind.

You who slumber still beneath the spell of matter, look beyond the descriptions of reality given by those who seek to lead you from without. Open to the living information of the life force that rises within you. This information is alive; *it is the only guidance you require.* At the deepest levels of your being you have always known these things. Behind your roles and societal illusions you are not separate from the source of life, nor are you cut off from the intelligence who, designing all form and structure, breathes into it the breath of life.

We who inhabit the fields of light share with you a common spirit. We knew you in the beginning—long before you dressed in robes of soil and stream. In oneness with you we sent forth the harmonic currents that brought this world to be. Together we parted the skies and opened the waters of the heavens. Where were you then if not with us? Together we formed the mountains and river valleys. Together we tapped the wellsprings of the deep. Together we poured our radiance into this world and quickened her creatures of water, earth, and sky. Come. Let us reunite. Brush away the dusty thoughts of a darker age.

Time and space do not revolve around humankind, but our dreams do, our plans do. We are depending on you to bring shape and texture to the order that has rested implicit within all Creation since before the first starry nebulae illumined dimensional space. We are inviting you to help us bring into physical formation the vision that inspires the universe.

Do you see, oh humans of this present world? Do you understand? *You are the template, the prototype of a new and universal species, part solar, part material, both temporal and eternal, the species that will span the gulf between the visible and invisible, bringing new worlds into form. Through you a new and unprecedented cycle of creation will occur.*

The awareness we call you toward lies far above the tangled circuits of linguistically structured thought. Its perceptions differ from your present and quickly passing cultural perceptions as greatly as the world of waking differs from the deepest midnight slumber.

7

Echoes of this awareness have ever haunted the historical continuum, surfacing here and there in your better music, glimmering occasionally in your finest art. But when you entertain the open and unbiased vision of eternity, even the best of what has been grows dim in the light of what you see. For in truth even the finest moments of the human past are but crude two-dimensional caricatures of the future that is soon to be.

2

Through Fields of Dreams

*T*o you it must seem long ago, the time before your embarkation, before you journeyed through the matter fields to surface on this world. But to us the hour is early still, and much will change before *our* morning has passed. You left us with instructions to bring you this record when the dawn was full. Come gather around this conscious fire, peoples of the earth, and listen to the spirits of the stars.

We would tell you of the early hours when your thoughts first came to rest upon this world, when your love first illumined the world and shone through robes of water and soil, days when we were with you yet, back when the world was young.

Eons ago, before there was physical matter, you were one with us. Your essence remains, even now, indistinguishable from the unified field of being out of which flow duality, multiplicity, and all that flourishes in the eternal play of polarities. In oneness with the Eternal Source, in flowing, fluid realms of all-spectrum light and love, we lived together in the early ages of the morning. Together we shared a common "I." As waves of energy, we flowed through fields of dreams, the landscape of our eternal home.

There was a game we would sometimes play, an elementary energy exchange, an early form of relationship. A segment of source energy would break itself free from the main body and assume momentary individuality, personifying selected frequencies in order to experience relationships with others who had done the same. From the realm of eternal unity we chose frequencies, hues, and rates of vibration. Like crystals of snow forming in a stratospheric cloud, we personified them in the field of our common being. Our locations created space, our movements, time.

The first personification of the Eternal One brought forth the second personification and instantaneously the third. For the very thought of coalescing consciousness into an "other" immediately evoked a definition of *One* that was not "one alone," but rather "one including other." In the Language of Light our word for "other" has no singular form, while both "one" and "infinity" are represented by the same word.

The Trinity we know as our source is not three beings alone, but three beings including within them all beings; its second and third persons contain the two primary divisions that include all creation. Its first person embraces the two and all that they contain, extending far beyond their dimensional worlds, so far beyond it cannot be conveyed in human terms.

The biases of human languages imply that there was a linear sequence to the unfoldment of the One through Trinity into multiplicity, but in reality this occurrence was and is as instantaneous as a thought, a thought intrinsic in the very nature of being, a thought that takes no time to appear. A thought, therefore, that has appeared many times before.

Throughout eternity, this thought comes into being again and again. While it is sustained, time also comes into being. When it is no longer animated, time ceases. The creation of specific beings or angels to sustain this thought over an open-ended stretch of time brought forth the steady stream of cumulative creation that has made possible, and given birth to, this present universe.

Though there is no linear sequence to the unfoldment of the One into the Trinity—and indeed, no linear sequence to the unfoldment of the Eternal Being into Cherubim and Seraphim, Thrones, Principalities, and multiple personifications of eternal spirit—a linear sequence of events did occur in the spirit world prior to the first physical manifestations of light, sound, and matter.

As a fetus experiences a gestation in the invisible realms before entering the stage of the visible world, so, too, do light, sound, galaxies, and all that they contain. Only after experiencing a cycle of development on the finer, more subtle frequencies of being, filling those realms to the full, do they spill over into physical objectification. In much the same way there was an invisible sequence of cause and effect that preceded your tumble into visible history. To rise again to your native levels of understanding, you must in a certain sense reverse that process.

You can reverse the process without conscious understanding. A child's trust in the inherent benevolence of life is all that is required. However, given your historical tendency to gravitate toward behavior based upon conceptual knowledge, it would be well for you to have at least some understanding of the decision that led you to inhabit the image worlds of these semiconscious primates.

If you are blessed with a child's trust and your mind does not trouble you with questions of how you came today to be so biologically clothed, move on to the chapters that follow this. Yet if a day comes when your mind needs to be calmed with a reminder of what it has not forgotten in its depths, know that a reminder is here for you, in this account.

If at any point in this narrative your spirit wants to fly more quickly than these words, move on. These words are offered to free you, to lift you. Skip over passages that may appear too detailed. They are for another time, if you need them, and only if you do. The weather is not the same today and tomorrow, and neither is the weather that keeps your conscious thought alive. On stormy days more detail will help you navigate true; you may then need these thoughts to fix your compass by. On days of sun and wind and open sea, the words you need to guide you are few. Take what thought you need today, but take no thought for tomorrow. Tomorrow you will not be the same. This much is sure.

These transmissions are designed to give you conceptual tools for those times you may need them, tools of insight to enhance your creative capacity and your enjoyment of the physical plane, tools that will reduce the likelihood of your sliding yet again into the sleep that has characterized this recent age.

To understand your fall into the troubled times of history, you must first recall the context in which it occurred.

The Fall from Awareness

Scattered throughout the sea of Eternal Being are distinct locations that radiate specific qualities. These qualities permeate the entire sea of creation, rippling throughout all that is, but the source locations from which they radiate are in either one of two constellations. These two constellations, Love and Truth, are two polarities of Eternal Being, two persons of the Trinity. They engender all that is. Their interplay evokes the universe and all the wonders it contains.

The Constellation of Love is the home of qualities associated with energy expression, and the Constellation of Truth is the home of qualities associated with form and structure. These two polarities overlap and interplay; neither is devoid of qualities originating in the other. The radiations of each quality permeate the entirety of both constellations, but the source from which each quality radiates is located in one constellation or the other.

Within this interplay between a constellation of qualities rooted in truth and a constellation of qualities rooted in love, individual spirit beings come into existence.

It is within this context that your current cycle of individuality began.

Each spirit being forms around specific frequency radiations of eternal qualities, consciously personifying them. Each individual spirit coalesces within the creative field that is generated by the interacting radiations of Love and Truth, and all things from the galaxies to the microbes are manifestations of these spirit beings; through them the universe comes into form.

There is no star in existence without a being who has chosen to appear as that star, nor is there any planet, asteroid, sun, or moon—no leaf, no insect, no flower, no tree, no tiny ocean snail, no grain of sand on the beach—that does not form around a spirit life.

When the first spirit beings—personifications of various qualities of awareness—would individualize and distinguish themselves from the main body of awareness to experience relationships with others who had done the same, they would after each relationship dissolve back again into the unity out of which they came. This process of individuation—spirits leaping dolphinlike from the sea of eternal unity into the air of individuality, then disappearing again beneath the waves of undifferentiated oneness—was purely for enjoyment. The first entities in the sea of being had no stake, no vested interest in their passing individual forms.

One day as you were individualizing certain qualities of eternal awareness, just emerging from a relationship, another entity of individualized awareness came to you and encouraged you to retain your present form of individuality and to carry that form over into a new relationship.

This was a new thought. It had never before occurred to you to experience multiple relationships without a renewal of identity.

13

You did not accept the idea immediately, but you did consider it. As you continued to listen, you mulled over its strange and fascinating possibilities. The curious being promoting this novelty appeared in a pulsing field of vibratory luminosity infinitely more beautiful and well defined than any you had ever seen. One of the attractive elements in this entity's proposal was that this path would, over time, allow the formation of the same sort of beautiful and intricate patterns within your own individualized field. But there was a dark side as well. Something else the entity said.

You were not entirely certain of its accuracy. At first you saw only humor in what seemed the absurdity of the thought. Yet as you considered it, you wondered if there might not be something to it. It took time and further argument, but eventually you were convinced by this entity that there was a possibility—perhaps even a strong one—that you might actually cease to exist if you did not follow this recommended course, consciously preserving your individuality from one relationship to the next. After all, you did not know exactly what happened to individuals who dissolved back into the sea . . .

This is the first lie that you believed.

The *form* of your individuality would, of course, cease to exist if your awareness were no longer focused through it, just as the focus of light through a lens ceases to exist when the light is turned in another direction. Yet the *potential* for your individuality would remain, just as the lens itself remains, should you again choose to turn your attention toward it. It would not disappear.

Potential can be either actualized or ignored, but it cannot be created or destroyed. All potential exists from the beginning and is eternal, as is the One whose being contains and sustains it.

You are reading these words at this moment through an individualized focus of your awareness, but *you* do not cease to exist with the cessation of that individuality. The awareness that shines through your lens of individuality is the awareness that shines through all lenses of individuality.

You are the being behind all individuals, the awareness within and beyond all these things. You know this in spirit. To know this while in individual form is to be conscious. To imagine that you are the focus of individuality itself, to imagine that you are the form and not the spirit that animates it is to be subconscious.

When any personification of eternal awareness (your own essential awareness) comes into a relationship with any other, it flows into a form of self-identity that will optimize creativity and enjoyment during the relationship. Just as an environment shapes and molds the plants that flourish within it, relationships mold the forms of identity for all healthy spirit beings. Since relationships are ever changing, healthy identities are ever changing as well, flowing from moment to moment, assuming the forms most suited to creative exchange.

In a healthy state, continuity of identity occurs on the level of spirit, not on the level of form.

Your fall from awareness of your eternal nature into the illusion of separation was not a single event. It was a gradual and, at first, a very subtle process. It began when you chose to retain a specific form of identity after the experience that had molded that identity had passed.

Choosing to bring a past-centered identity into a present experience reduced your sensitivity to the influences of the new moment. The new relationship could no longer guide your sense of self into identity patterns conducive to optimal interaction. Consequently, as you will see more clearly as our account progresses, your very presence was reduced along with the clarity of your perception.

You quickly found that an identity based on memory of the past had to be consciously sustained. Unlike natural, healthy identities, which formed and dissolved without conscious effort, an arbitrary, past-oriented sense of self required maintenance. You began to take yourself more seriously.

You began to think of yourself more as the external *form* of expression and less as the *spirit* behind expression. You began to give your individual identity greater importance than was its due. You overlooked something vital: You forgot that you have the ability to individualize the quality of self perfect for each occasion. Overriding the natural process through which your sense of self spontaneously flows into organic expression, your presence, though in reality still coming from the Eternal Source, was no longer a clear extension of that Source. Yet this was very subtle at first, merely a slight off-center shift of emphasis.

After a time of many relationships upon the higher frequencies of the spirit world, you traveled with the others of your Light Circle toward the central region of the Constellation of Truth, the region known as the Fields of Structure. You entered the awesome and wonderful realms where the processes of materialization were occurring. In the Fields of Structure, the thoughts in which you conceived yourself gradually began to draw to them the tiny crystallized particles that blew up from the Region of Stars far below.

Many of us have gone through this materialization process consciously, identifying with matter only when we chose, keeping our original sense of spirit self intact, remaining integral, whole, holy, connected with the Great Spirit, acquiring material clothing for purposes of creation and enjoyment, but never forgetting ourselves, never confusing the wearer of the robe with the fabric of the robe. But your habits of identity were such that this was not your experience. As particles of matter were drawn to your biogravitational thought fields, you began identifying with what was becoming an increasingly tangible form.

As they were gradually clothed in successive layers of molecular structure, you began to see the thoughts of individuality that you had chosen to hold beyond their time. You were fascinated. They were very beautiful.

Within the luminous field of energy that distinguished the focus of your attention, a body began to take shape. The first particles that gave it form were extremely fine and subtle, smaller than the finest molecules. You identified with the swirling patterns they formed within your energy field, these early forerunners of cells and organs.

Until this point, your central motivation had always been love. It is true that it had been qualified from time to time by a sense of curiosity that was not always in your best interests, but there was an innocence about it and certainly no selfish or fearful intent. Even as your etheric body formed within you, your motivation remained primarily centered in love.

But as you played around the edges of the Fields of Structure and identified with ever more tangible and beautiful sheaths of shimmering individuality, you would occasionally entertain in your consciousness a whispering of doubt, a whispering so effervescent, so subtle, so much at the periphery of your thoughts that you hardly noticed it at first.

"I am supported by this sea," whispered the doubt, "this sea of universal being, but what if someday it is no longer here? Will its support always continue? Will it sustain my awareness forever? Does it care for my individuality? For these beautiful forms and patterns that my thoughts are creating within me? These patterns are what make me unique. I have been watching them for so long, I am not entirely sure anymore what I would be without them. What if this sea of being, great and benevolent though it is, were to dislike my growing sheath of tangibility? What if a time comes when the sea is gone and I find myself alone?"

As time passed this whispering became so familiar that you assumed such thoughts were your own. Already confusing your sense of self with the thought formations that swirled within your awareness, you now began to feel protective toward those formations, to feel anxiety for them—and for yourself. So it was that you entered the astral realms,

17

identifying not only with prior thought and experience but also with emotional energy patterns that did not always originate in the pure currents of perfect love.

The knowledge that the others of your Light Circle were focalizations of the same awareness you knew as your own gradually began to fade. For the first time, you began to perceive "others" who did not seem to have emerged from your own root being. Actually, these others were beings just like yourself. Some would complete their courses and return in time to the field of unity, but others were gathering layers of experience without the natural relinquishing of form that characterizes and renews all healthy identities. Like you, they soon found that tension was required to hold on to their images and memories.

They also found it increasingly difficult to distinguish these past impressions from their sense of self. They lost contact with the creative currents of renewal that are designed to recharge periodically all aware creatures, keeping them clear-sighted, alert, and in communion with the Source. Simultaneously, these entities, and there were many of them by now, found themselves growing bodies of increasingly dense form.

Meanwhile, there were others of us in these fields of dreams who watched this behavior from afar. We saw many of the playful, happy beings whom we knew as our companions and friends, one by one, becoming dull, serious, afraid. It seemed to us that a branch of our family had been infected with some strangely debilitating perceptual disorder. We attempted to communicate telepathically with them as we did with one another, but we found that we did not understand the strangely biased dialects of their now significantly altered thought processes.

They thought our inability to communicate with them was due to our ignorance. Eventually they lost interest in what they came to regard as the "ethereal opinions of insubstantial entities." Yet we could see growing dis-ease and unhappiness recorded ever more graphically in their developing bodies. We saw clearly what they could no longer see: the inevitable danger that awaited them if they continued to follow such ever-narrowing identity beams all the way to their inevitable conclusion.

Among those of us who wanted to offer assistance were some who realized that we could only speak to them in their own terms, through material forms similar enough to their own to elicit their notice and respect. These beings, Angels of Principality (or Bodhisattvas, as they are called in some traditions) decided to embark on a course of *conscious* materialization. We watched them enter the Fields of Structure and spiral downward, only to see appearing in many of them, too, the darkening of luminosity and crystallization of imagery that characterized those whom they had hoped to help.

Yet despite the contagious nature of the disorder, a few among the Principalities escaped contamination. These few proceeded all the way down the whirlpool-like energy vortex of gathering structure with a unified sense of identity still prevailing in their awareness. We watched them spiral around and around, side by side with the others, circling ever downward through increasingly lower frequencies, accumulating more tangible material dress with the deepening levels of their descent.

It was a race of sorts, the conscious Principalities attempting to beat the fearful to materialization upon the physical plane. The conscious Principalities arrived first.

In a forest-covered river valley upon this very earth at the edge of a fertile plain they took on the luminous garments of the first human biology. Though their uncontested stewardship of this region of the earth was brief by eternal standards, it was nevertheless sufficient to see the Creator's intentions flow through human form into the creation of exquisite fruit, vegetation, and animal species. From this time have arisen the human myths and legends of paradise. As the legends also recall, this era was not to last.

All too soon, it seemed, the dark Principalities arrived, angry at the disease they had acquired and at those in whom it had originated. Shortly after them arrived the many entities like yourself. Not long after your arrival on the physical plane you began to think of yourself as separate beings, cut off, distinct from your source. You developed a strange habit of storing identities within your psyche as one might store dresses or suits of clothing in a closet, preserving them with herbs of self-importance and spices of fear.

Your overall awareness was still predominantly centered in the currents of love; you were certainly not "evil" at this point. For many centuries you continued to share the same equatorial region of the earth both with the fallen Principalities and with Principalities who had not lost their eternal awareness, all of you in human form. You knew times of great joy and happiness as well as times of doubt and confusion. Yet with each additional passage of the moon the implications of your overidentification with form appeared more and more forcefully around you.

3

Angels of the Primal Coherence

Twenty billion years of unfoldment leave this universe yet in its early stages. It is still a realm of vast extremes: frozen worlds of rigid matter contrasting the awesome heat of stars—with light years of empty space between. What biology there is appears only as a slight and nearly indistinguishable film on the surface of but a few worlds. Yet in that biological film lies the future.

It is a relatively new substance, biology. Its day has only now begun to dawn. The present universal distribution of matter, time, space, and energy forms but the skeletal structure of what is to be. As the galaxies spiral, so the linear progressions of creation spiral as well, until the passage of change brings to this great Universal Medicine Wheel the forms that have ever lain dormant within. For these galaxies are nests and pods. Each of their fiery stars is a seed, with inherent designs yet to be released as distinct from what stars are today as the acorn is distinct from the oak.

Within and suspended among the stars of each galactic nest, eternal intent radiates fields of energy not visible to your physical sight. These fields of energy are called into being by the vibrational structure of the primal sound, the first tone or word. "In the beginning was the Word, and the Word was with God and the Word was God."

Just as vegetation grows up along the life-giving network of a river's water, the physical forms of the future develop along these circuits of primal sound. As the universe unfolds, the circuits attract the beings and design patterns that objectify the creative intentions of the One who is the giver of life.

Within the parameters of these energy circuits, individual beings are free to choose from among infinite role possibilities those that best suit them and their natures. They are free to improvise their unique harmonic styles of creation within the frequencies of the word. The word's enfolded order is invisible to physical sight, but through the eyes of spirit it can be seen.

If you close your eyes you may see it stretching before you: a pulsing network of implicit potential as real as any sensory realm, a vibrational reality that in an earlier age was called the kingdom of heaven. It is the spatial—but not yet temporal—objectification of universal thought designs, a world of metaform and archetype, a realm of intention waiting to materialize.

It is the spiritual scaffold around which the biology of the future will congeal into a work of splendor and magnificence *without precedent and, as yet, without name*. It is a blueprint, a subtle latticework of intent and vibration; it is the outline, the pattern for a finely woven, luminous biology of galactic and someday intergalactic extent.

Through you the potential of this implicit order will one day dance to life. New beings, new creatures will appear to fly among the fields of what is now still formless space, to share with us the joys of universal exploration. One day you will call into orbital patterns the atoms, molecules, and cells that will objectify this infrastructure and provide its physicality. But perhaps you sense it now, perhaps you feel already the awakening. We address you now upon the frequencies of your essence, to remind you, to help you recall.

The time you create spirals outward from your presence like a ship's wake trailing through the ocean. The immediate past fans out behind you. In its fertile cone, life appears in many forms; in it, the earth has seen a biosphere flourish. Yet it is not the past that reveals your direction, but the purpose with which you move. The cone of your future intentionality spirals brilliant and multidimensional before you, illuminating the universal potential that will one day take form. Like the light of a radiant beacon, it reveals your vibrational sketchings in the heavens.

From your center in Eternal Being, energy intent swirls outward to become beings, individualized forms of your expression: angels, pattern beings, generations of light. Issuing from the heart of this dimensional creation, your intelligence radiates outward in concentric pulsations, rippling throughout the far-flung fields of space. At the simultaneous velocity of love it is multiplied in the transforming prism of each galactic core. From the center of each galaxy your intelligence flows outward to each star and multiplies again. And on the process goes: From the center of this sun star it flows to the earth and into the awakening human cells of the earth's nearly activated planetary nervous system.

Your multiplications of consciousness call forth the linearity of time, even as the many beings sharing your consciousness bring the passages of the moon about the earth, the earth around the sun, and the sun in a spiral cluster with others of its kind.

Your movement now brings this star system into a new region of space. You stationed us here, Angels of the Primal Coherence, to remind you, to awaken you. "Lest in sleeping, I forget," you said. "Lest in dreaming a planetary creation I become lost in the wonders of time."

In this quarter century, your dream produces its harvest. The bridge between Creator and Creation appears. A human family awaits your conscious habitation. The intelligence overridden and denied in the historical state awakens as a sleeper awakening within a single body. It circulates through human minds, looks through human eyes, interprets the world through human forms. And it knows itself as one.

The field of collective human consciousness is now entering the final stage of the awakening process, congealing into awareness of itself as the organ of consciousness (similar in function to a brain) of *a single planetary being*, a being with internal organs of oceans, forests, ecosystems, and atmosphere. Humankind is its system both for processing information and for directing its future development.

The language through which we are currently filtering these thoughts has no adequate words for this single planetary being, for the Creator, or even for the human species. We choose the nearest approximate labels, hoping that the structure in which we weave these thoughts will penetrate below the surface of your mind to reveal a sense of the underlying rhythms of awareness behind them, stirring your own perception and memory and providing you, from within, an understanding, an experience deeper and more comprehensive than these words alone can provide. The purpose of these transmissions is to awaken the Creator upon this material world—and to guide *you* into that awakening awareness.

The Currents of Universal Awareness

One intelligence flows through all creatures, but as it is channeled it is focused in many different ways through the various dimensional levels, like high-voltage current moving through a series of step-down transformers. In posthistoric societies of the earth, human thought and activity will be guided by that intelligence in one or another of its various forms. Certain creative acts will bring, through human form,

galactic intelligence, others the universal intelligence that or-
chestrates the galactic network itself. The varying needs of
each creative situation will call for people to draw upon different types and qualities of awareness.

Through some the awakened planetary intelligence of
the earth will flow, while at the same time others will be
conduits for the solar intelligence of this star system—or perhaps at times, the intelligence of other stars. Many will channel the intelligence of that Being who is the catalyst and
creator of all biological life.

Yet the varieties of universal intelligence are not limited
to just its larger focalizations. When it is helpful or required,
people in posthistoric times will also represent the intelligence of the angelic beings associated with specific
bioregions, with rivers, lakes, and mountains, or if it is helpful, with the animal and vegetable life forms of the earth.
Even the intelligence of atomic and molecular structure will
be invoked, consulted, and utilized in creative activities
where it is relevant.

Healthy human individuality brings with it a *hologramatic* understanding of the Being whose unfoldment is
this universe, *an understanding in which the whole is microcos-
mically reflected in the structure of the part.*

To activate this understanding, to access the many frequencies of its awareness, you have only to recall, to notice
your primal union with the Source of life, the Source of *your*
life, and to elevate that union to the citadel of your decision
making. When you understand the nature of your essential
being in metapersonal terms, you know your human body as
a cell in a developing planetary organism. And you recognize in that organism the signature of your own spiritual
identity.

In much the same way that complete genetic information for an entire human body is contained in each of the
body's many trillion cells, each awakened human being has
inner access to the information circulating in the unified field
of awareness that precedes all individuality.

Wherever the symphonic rhythms of the universal dance pervade, each part within each larger unit experiences this sort of hologramatic relationship to the whole. Consequently, when you live in a harmonic state your consciousness provides you with options not available to those who imagine themselves existing in isolation.

To know yourself as an awakened individual is to also know yourself as *the being of the surrounding context.*

When you are not focused on the creative or interpretative enjoyment of individuality, you are free to experience the organic identity shift that brings awareness of your larger collective humanity. In the same way, you are free to shift through connection with humankind's collective "I" into an experience of planetary identity, solar identity, or identity as the great spiraling being of the Milky Way.

In posthistoric times you will know each level of creative manifestation as a dimension, or octave, of your own being's unfoldment. You will experience naturally the freedom and mobility of musically directed travel up and down these octaves of manifestation.

You cannot travel into yourself without exploring the infinite reaches of eternal consciousness.

You cannot know yourself in reality without knowing God.

Each plane of manifestation is a higher octave on a single vibrational continuum. The lower octaves offer greater multiplicity and a greater diversity of creation. With the higher octaves comes reduced multiplicity and a more intensified awareness of the singularity of being. Yet this generalization applies only to the landscape of Creation. It does not apply to you. You are able to move freely where you will.

You have long enjoyed descending in full consciousness through successively lower octaves, thereby multiplying beings of diversity and, through them, your own cocreative opportunities. Since the creation of this universal landscape, at each level of your descent you have appeared as individual beings designed to interact with, and create upon, the frequencies of each octave in turn.

The physical plane is the lowest of the seven higher or primary planes of manifestation. It is the densest of the conscious planes and the lowest octave in which you have sought to incarnate in multiple forms while simultaneously sustaining awareness of your unified field. While the beings appearing on the higher, nonphysical frequencies all naturally assumed a healthy hologramatic understanding of their origin in you, on the physical level among the biologically incarnate this understanding has not been continuous. It has faded in and out, flickering and blurring.

Human reception of eternal awareness has been poor, at times even curtailed by the separatist nature of the self-images of historical peoples. You naturally seek to awaken in them the same sort of healthy hologramatic self-understanding that is experienced by the beings of higher, less substantial frequencies, but humankind's extreme overidentification with form requires that such an awakening be gradual. You do not want to dissolve their individual distinctions in a single burst as they realize their essential unity with you and the singular field of our common awareness. For such a sudden change in self-understanding could dissolve their individual body fields. And your goal is not to end individuality but to inhabit it.

So you have sought to awaken humans slowly over the centuries, preserving their self-distinctions that they might continue with you as a family, as a cooperative association of interconnected informational beings.

Breaking through into the collective field of human consciousness and then sustaining that breakthrough during this past cycle of education has required all your humor and wisdom and that of your angelic legions for many thousands of years.

Guiding collective human thought toward the currents of universal awareness has been slow and tedious. We have long known that the larger the earth's human population, the greater the probability of awakening. Yet for millennia, territorial fear-centered behavior has kept human numbers reduced to so few that genuine breakthroughs—sustained spirit incarnations—were extremely rare.

The development of greatest relevance in recent centuries has been the consistent, and in this century, dramatic, improvement in the field of intrahuman communication. As a result of new human communication technology, our work of education was able to leap forward rapidly. Our initial efforts to use the print medium for the distribution of health-related information were not entirely successful in the face of ecclesiastical opposition and an extremely low overall rate of literacy. But health awareness eventually did spread and human populations have since multiplied accordingly.

Meanwhile, the predisposition toward awakening has grown at a rate more rapid than the population, and our continuing inspiration of better and more effective communication tools has resulted in technology that currently unites the diverse human cultures of the earth in a single global communications network. Our educational activities become more conscious and more effective with each passing day.

The worst-case scenarios for transition into the posthistoric order are no longer likely. In some cases they are no longer possible. And our education is continuously reducing the likelihood of scenarios of lesser destruction. It is actually possible—not quite likely yet, but possible—that we might yet achieve our optimal goal of a smooth and peaceful transition. A chain reaction in human understanding resulting in planetary awakening could theoretically occur at any time.

On the eve of this great metahistorical event, the current of universal attention is flowing so powerfully toward this imminent awakening that it resembles a river approaching floodtide. Throughout the realms where those of our kind are conscious, we share this awesome current of attention. As creatures of the current, we qualify its interests with our individuality, working together in our various capacities to help you awaken to your native understanding.

Your awakening, when complete, will signal a distinct new evolutionary phase, with new ground rules and wholly altered creative conditions.

4

Behind the Historical Disorder

*T*here are some in your present human world who, having achieved a partial memory of their own pattern of incarnation, conclude that the descent into biological form would not have occurred had it not been for excessive fear and overidentification with the past; yet this is not the case. Incarnation into biological form was intended from the beginning.

As incarnation into biological form occurred, each spirit could have remained fully conscious of its eternal nature and its hologramatic relationship to the Eternal Source—indeed, a few spirits did remain conscious of this. Your fragmentation and your overidentification with an exclusive sense of self distorted your process of incarnation. However, it did not cause it.

You—and others of your Light Circle—had long before chosen to spearhead the Eternal One's exploration and development of the material universe.

Your fall into fearful thought and nonfluid patterns of identity was not mere happenstance. An influence encouraged you in this direction, encouraged you to identify with an exclusive sense of separate self. With the exception of the

Luminous Principalities, those angels who were the first to incarnate humanly, virtually all members of your race fell under the spell of this influence at some point during their journeys into biological form. We call this influence the *materializing influence,* or when speaking in the plural, the forces of materialization.

The materializing influence is the force of specified definition. It plays a central role in the creation and sustenance of the dimensional universe. Like frost drawing individualized ice crystals from the air, this influence draws crystallizations of basic molecular structure from the omnipresent energy currents of eternal love.

The materializing influence is the principle of contraction that holds energy efficiently bound in matter. It guides the internal dynamics of matter and energy distribution in stars as well as the thermal and geological processes of planets like the earth. It is the quintessential materializing principle at its most basic level.

This influence is personified, as are all qualities and influences in this potent universe. In the West, both the influence itself and its personifications have been referred to as Satan. Yet stereotypical images of Satan have prevented many people from understanding the real nature of the materializing principle. Satan is the personified principle that rules the background landscape of Creation, as well as the many highly focused elemental beings who work together to regulate the systems and processes of materiality.

These universally systemic beings are the Creator's means of keeping material structure—that is, all energy patterns without the individualized selfhood that comes with personal will—in assigned patterns of form and behavior. They are the caretakers of Creation's landscape, the rulers of subconscious processes and events. Together they implement the laws that maintain the universal landscape. Mechanical laws, physical laws, gravitational, electrical, magnetic, thermal, atomic, subatomic, temporal, and spatial laws are all regulated by the materializing forces. In these, *the subconscious realms,* the materializing forces function as intended. They carry out their roles with precision and efficiency.

You realized when you initiated this human project that the forces of materialization would play some role in developing the values of your incarnating spirits, but just how extensive a role was difficult to estimate, for in the *conscious realms* the determination of value depends entirely on individual choice. The nature of human design required that the optimal ratio between spirit (energy) values and material (matter) values come from the incarnate ones themselves. Since they were creatures of free will it could not be imposed or legislated. They alone—from within their biological forms—could determine the optimal spirit/matter balance.

For the completed human species to serve as a conscious link between Creator and Creation, it was essential that its development be influenced by material values as well as by values of spirit. To actualize your vision of a species through whom you would one day explore the material universe and develop the universe's potential, at the end of its developmental cycle this race would have to be a product of both spirit and soil in equal balance.

This could not happen if you were to remain fully conscious throughout the descent of your individual spirits into material bodies, for the necessary material complementation would then be insufficient, and the requisite spirit/matter balance would be absent. The dissipation, or relaxation, of your unified field of awareness during the cycle when human beings were multiplying upon the earth was the only way the completed race would emerge sufficiently grounded in the physical plane to serve effectively as a bridge between spirit and matter.

And so you chose to sleep for a while, allowing the materializing influences to flow freely in and around the developing species. But while your sleep itself was intended, the excessive dominance of materiality during humankind's development was not.

The Excessive Dominance of Materiality

During the cycle of human development, the materializing influence was intended to engender human understanding of the basic laws pertaining to matter. It was intended to instill in humankind necessary material-plane sensibilities. For the larger percentage of your conscious thought and the conscious thought of the humans who hologramatically shared your awareness to remain available for creation and discovery, the organ of consciousness that humankind was growing into was designed to have its basic life-support functions served by autonomic systems. Since the forces of materialization regulate all subconscious processes, these autonomic systems would naturally fall under their jurisdiction.

It was here that your margin of error was exceeded.

There is quite a difference in playing a role in subconscious human processes and in dominating conscious human decision making. While the one was intended, the other was not.

Before the initiation of the human project, the materializing forces had always received their instructions directly from the field of awareness that was their Creator and source. However, anticipating the nature of the highly specified biological creation you one day intended to produce while incarnate in human form, just before you dissolved your unified field identity you extended the jurisdiction of the forces of materialization to include any future directives that you might issue through incarnate human beings.

While continuing in their current roles, you instructed the entities associated with the forces of materialization to honor all human requests for their regulatory services. This is where the misunderstanding occurred.

Your traditions consider the entities associated with the materializing principle—Satan and his legions—evil. Yet in their proper sphere of influence, these beings are necessary and essential elements of the material worlds. The decisive current of instructive energy they utilize to govern atomic and molecular formation is not evil when interacting with matter and its many structures; *it is the very current of divine design.* The materializing influence only becomes evil (or destructive) when it enters the sphere of human decision making. There it translates into myopic, fear-centered logic that is not compatible with the more expansive awareness for which humankind is designed.

How did the forces of materialization come to influence human consciousness? At one time or another, they must have received nearly every conceivable request from someone in human form, requests they were bound to honor. This brought their influence into regions of human consciousness, where it was never intended to be.

The result has been the virtual domination of historical human consciousness by excessively materialistic values. The resulting static has interfered with human reception of those frequencies of eternal awareness that were intended to guide them.

While it is appropriate for materialistic values to dominate atomic and subatomic realms, they become extremely destructive when they dominate human determination. For they effectively move the whole seat of decision making from the eternal awareness of spirit to the individual's accumulated knowledge of good and evil. The fearful logic and tendencies toward exaggeration that accrue from this misappropriated influence have caused the confusion in human understanding that has led to these past millennia of history. They have led many of your incarnating spirits into forms of self-understanding that correspond to neither your intentions nor reality.

Under the dominance of the materializing influence—or "the spell of matter"—many of the early human incarnations came to discredit their own perspectives, doubting their source and validity. Since they were designed to be guided by these, their own views, discrediting them was like destroying one of their primary senses. They blinded themselves spiritually. They were perceiving a seven-dimensional physical planet in three dimensions.

Understandably, without their primary means of terrestrial guidance, they began to encounter navigational difficulties. These difficulties only confirmed the doubts they had regarding the validity of their inherent spiritual perception. Quickly, they lost the self-confidence that, like a gyroscope, was designed to stabilize their eternal awareness while incarnate in biological form.

Mistrusting their own perception, they began placing exaggerated emphasis on the experience and perception of others. They assigned spirit credibility *externally*, where it had no place. Ultimately, they believed the influences coming from outside themselves were more real than the influence coming from the presence of God within them. Believing lies, they exchanged their beautifully unique individuality for conformity to a fear-centered external code.

Though it would not be until the end of the historical gestation process that your unified field would again be activated, awakening humankind to a common field of awareness, your species was intended to remain conscious of their eternal spirits throughout their multiplication and flourishing on the earth. Since you had given the spirits incarnating in human form jurisdiction over the forces of materialization, you had assumed that incarnating spirits would accurately assess the appropriate extent of the materializing influence and regulate it accordingly.

It had occurred to no one that they might so overemphasize the values associated with sensory impressions that they would forget their eternal origins and, thus, their purpose for taking on human form.

It was natural that sensory input would have to be assigned a proper place in the value system of each newly incarnate one, natural that it might even dominate for a time while adjustments were made. But the possibility was not anticipated that sensory interpretations might block out all other awareness in some entities, curtailing even their very memory of self, fostering a period of historical amnesia during which whole human societies would degenerate into barbarism and savagery.

Nor was it necessary.

Since their origin as individualized entities on the higher frequencies of Eternal Being, the spirits incarnating into human form have been gifted with complete freedom of will. Their original fall from consciousness was no more necessary then than the daily repetition of it is now.

Awakening from the Spell of Matter

The fall has no power or momentum of its own; it must be regenerated daily. And it is within each individualized spirit cell, within your own individualized spirit and ego, on an intimate and immediate level, that you must recognize and correct this imbalance if you are to help us in the education and healing of your world.

For while you are the whole, you are also each one sleeping in your collective soul, and wherever one yet sleeps in history's stormy dream, so too sleeps that part of you. If you are conscious in the one who reads these words, move on now past these next few pages. Resume the thread where it sparkles and gives words to what you know. But if you have slumbered recently, or feel yet confused, these words speak to you.

It is vital that you recognize the fall for what it is: *a lack of trust* that has become habitual, culturally encoded, and passed on from one generation to the next.

To doubt yourself is to doubt the wisdom and viability of the human design. To fully trust in God you must also trust yourself. No one is created without everything required to make healthy, wholesome decisions.

The fall is regenerated each time you doubt your ability to meet creatively the challenges of life, each time you turn your back on your inherent understanding and seek to replace it with the inferior images and beliefs peddled by the deities of the historical condition.

History has many deities, many false gods, many *patterns of orientation* that are destructive to the human spirit and incompatible with your eternal nature. Chief among these have been fear, reason, social convention, and tradition. Each of these can be valuable and useful *in your service;* however, when you serve them, they become extremely destructive.

The patterns of orientation that emerge from time to time as history's deities are *goods exaggerated into evils* by those whose awareness is dominated by the materializing influence.

When dominant in human consciousness, the materializing influence clouds human perception. The people under its spell can no longer see clearly. They take something— tradition, for example—that is designed as an occasionally helpful behavioral guide *within the context of their lives* and they turn it into the context itself. What was designed as a convenience for their conscious use becomes inflated into a structure that instead dominates all that they do.

The materializing influence, in its proper place, is no more evil than the force you use to pick up an apple or plant a seed, but when conscious entities open their awareness to its slower subconscious frequencies, they experience the decisive currents that rule there as fear, and for them the experience is hell, because conscious beings were designed to function with an awareness diametrically opposed to the awareness that maintains subconscious formations.

People have the prerogative of entering such subconscious frequencies; however, this locks them into awareness patterns that do not include a full field of perception, awareness patterns that, technically speaking, are subhuman. Unable to comprehend why a benevolent God would create a hell, many deny the existence of such a place. Yet every creature by nature of its design has an intended range of function. It is hell for a fish to be on dry land, hell for a bird to be confined in a cage. Similarly, hell is a daily experience wherever people are motivated by currents of fear that were intended to play only peripheral roles in their lives.

When human beings accept fear into their lives as a primary motivational current, the resulting static clouds their reception of the higher frequencies, shutting out both eternal awareness and the energy currents that bring love and beauty into the world. They then find themselves so preoccupied with the projections of their imaginations that they are virtual prisoners of their own designs. They feel cramped and confined, frustrated, confused. They see little but their own interpretations. This is historical reality. At its best it offers hints and promises of splendid and awesome possibilities to come. At its worst it is a continuation of the only hell there ever was or ever will be.

There is no gray area to your behavioral choices, no shadowy realm where you are partly in the new reality and partly without. There are specific frequencies on which you are designed to function, frequencies that are native to you, as other frequencies are native to other creatures. You either function on those frequencies or you do not.

To use your free will to choose to function on frequencies for which you were not designed brings bondage, not freedom.

Concepts and ideologies that are rooted in fear, even arbitrarily maintained belief systems that on the surface may not appear to be rooted in fear, act as shields to block out the emanations of eternity. They surround those who believe in them, generating what for all intents and purposes is an impervious dome, an effective invisible barrier through which the currents of universal thought cannot pass. They block the individual's awareness of the perceptual frequencies that alone can give them the insight they need to be themselves.

Ideologies are toxic. They poison perception and happiness. They block access to the intelligence that is designed to guide people's lives.

To choose religious or ideological dogmatism in the name of freedom is as foolish as for a jailed man to exercise his right to remain in prison. To choose bondage may be the familiar choice, the traditional choice, but it is fatal all the same. It is the choice of subconsciousness over consciousness, the choice of mortality over eternal life, the very choice responsible for all the heartache and suffering of human history.

The choice to function on the love-centered motivational frequencies, where you are designed to function, is the only choice that brings freedom. It does not limit you to a predetermined script but offers a range of behavior that evokes your fullest potential. The historically programmed have but a few cultural selections before them, while the improvisational options that open before you as you ride the energy currents of eternal love are infinitely varied. You are free again to share with us the joy and challenge that comes with habitation of a sensuous universe.

Though it can take many forms, in human consciousness the materializing influence appears primarily as a pattern of convoluted logic that encourages fear-centered thought and can lead to self-destructive behavior. This influence is being driven out of human consciousness by the intensifying energy field generated as the collective awakening proceeds. Even as these words are shared, the self-serving, the promoters of human fear, those given over to greed and manipulation are experiencing a loss of personal vitality, as a direct consequence of the withdrawal of this influence. They are being challenged to change their understanding of self and world, to stop relating to a fictitious realm of presumed "others," and to relax back into the rich interconnectivity of the loving matrix that gave them birth. They are being invited to know themselves as parts of an integral planetary organism.

To you who place your trust in the gentle wisdom that, behind all cultural conditioning, continues even now to provide the current of your awareness, to you who trust your-selves, history's deities are transformed into agents of excellence.

In their rightful places they will serve you long and well, as will the materializing forces from which they draw their patterns of structure. They are cruel and terrible masters to the hesitant and the doubtful, but they deeply respect and are most eager to serve those who carry the consciousness of eternity. You have the authority and the knowledge to assign them to tasks of your choosing—an easy matter, when you think of it, a detail. But an important detail.

For by assigning fear and its offspring to creative roles in your service, you remove the materializing influence from the field of your conscious awareness. You emerge from the spell of matter, setting up a powerful resonance, a morphogenetic field that radiates outward from your heart, penetrating the surrounding atmosphere, making it easier for others also to reorient in love.

No matter how well you may understand this on a spirit level—and of course in spirit you do understand—you must bring your ego into that understanding and practice this truth, live with it on a daily basis, or your awakening is not complete.

Your challenge is to awaken from the spell of matter while still retaining the human forms you have gathered about you during your descent into this physical world. Our legions are here to encourage and support you. We remember your instructions from the moment before you scattered into the seeds of humanity. Even as we watched your many individuations drifting downward in the spiral dances of gathering structure, your words rang in our ears.

"Wake me," you said, "that I might arise in the forms that emerge at this journey's end, and through them bestow my gifts upon this world. Join me then in the matter fields, that together we might work to magnify the beauty and the wonder of these physical domains."

Within you who read these words, that vision swirls, latent in a burning love for the productions of time, a love that we now call upon you to remember as your own.

Within you slumbers the creative vision that first illumined dimensional space. Within you the Star Maker trembles on the threshold of awakening. Your ego will not dissolve in such an awakening; it will ascend into enlightened comprehension of its cocreative partnership with the Eternal Being in whom this universe congeals. Already you are moving in the currents of eternal thought. As you continue to flow with this thought, it becomes your own. You remember.

5

The Transmutation of Error

It is neither possible nor desirable to avoid all painful or sorrowful experiences during the course of incarnation, but in most of the human cultures that have passed across the earth all but a small percentage of such experiences could have been avoided.

Just as in the past individuals made the decisions that resulted in the deflection of human energy into the historical detour, so in this age it is individuals who break the patterns of history and light the passageways of understanding that lead back to consciousness of eternal life.

Decisions are not made by races, cultures, or nations, unless they are first made by individuals. *The most destructive decision that an individual can make is to give away his or her decision-making authority.*

The decision that lies at the source of human history is the decision through which you have given away your power to the very forces you came here to regulate. We have been weaning you and your race away from this tendency, away from this willingness to give away your power, for tens of thousands of years.

Human history has been a process of increasing decision-making responsibility on the part of the individual. It is the story of declining aristocracies and the diminishing power of elites. It is the record of tyranny's demise, a chronology of the dismantling of hierarchical structures. As far back as your records go, they document the steady growth of individual rights and individual responsibility.

These most recent centuries bring this process into stark and vivid highlight with the final breakup of feudalism and the birth of democracy, socialism, and other forms of government, which, for all their failures, nevertheless honor principles of collective value and conduct.

Though the fall has had a severe effect on humankind's enjoyment and understanding during this past age, it has not critically inhibited the development of the species. Physically, genetically, and biologically, humankind has continued to develop much as originally intended.

Whenever there were deviations from the optimal patterns of development, they have always been used profitably. In the end there is not one moment that does not contribute in some way toward perfection. Even at those critical junctures where the optimal path was not taken, if you follow the tale further down the path that was chosen you find that, though its course twists and winds, it returns eventually not merely to the original path but to a level of perfection one octave higher on the spiral of creative unfoldment.

In electrical circuitry the shortest distance between two points is rarely the best way for the current to flow. If the current in a radio flowed directly from the power source to the speaker, there would be no reproduction of sound. The radio's diversion of electrical energy into purposeful circuitry creates the framework that makes possible both its reception of invisible waves and its translation of those waves into meaningful sound.

This same principle applies to the realms of material circuitry. The shortest distance between two points is always *creative* in the sense that energy is released and utilized in some way, for some purpose, but it is not always the most desirable or most creative route for the energy to travel. When the pure energy of the life force follows the shortest route to the heart of matter, stars are born. But to actualize and then to stabilize the biological possibilities of a cool, water-heavy world, the energies of life do not take the shortest route—they detour through mazelike and life-forming circuitry.

The creation of an organ of biological consciousness made up of many billion human individuals, each hologramatically conscious of the whole, is a process involving many steps, incorporating many overlapping layers of biological order. It has required the elaborate weaving of precise patterns of circuitry in environments designed to draw forth the required forms, attitudes, values, talents, attributes, and passions. To be of service to this world's completed biological organ of consciousness, constituent human beings must be not merely attuned to the rhythms and energy pulsations of the whole but also participating in them freely, of their own will. Without voluntary participation the associations of diverse cells that you know as organisms would not be possible. Therefore, the experience, whatever form it takes, that brings human beings to the realization that it is in their interest to cooperate with universal intent and design is all part of the process.

Some of the circuitry that has been created in human experience has been unnecessary. It has involved sagas, tales, and histories that were less than enjoyable for those involved. But all of this ultimately will be turned to advantage. Nothing is lost in the process.

There is a profound and objective intelligence aware of the flutter of every insect wing—observing, noting, assigning, and enfolding all life. And what is true of an insect's wing as it turns to catch the sun is true of you. And of all.

Even during history's darkest hour:

In perfect love's economy
tragedy, catastrophe
are retranslated for those who pass
instantaneous, accurate
dispassionate
in terms of light and sound
until, *and so,*
they know
why they chose that.

Not a sparrow has fallen to the ground
not a thought more consciously
gently laid to rest.
No human life was ever lost.

Live, lost souls, live on
for you know how they thought you gone
and how ascending free you've flown.
Live, lost souls, live on

For the beauty, the wonder,
the magic you have known.

6

Generations of Light

As spirals of white, circling slower, and deeper spirals of turquoise and aquamarine, we see the moon's rotations around this world—flowing streams of liquid light, continuous to our slower sight, woven spirals of earth and moon, sailing around and around the rainbow spirals of this nearest star. Your sun is no stationary light but rides swiftly with its whirling worlds through a moving arm of a spiral galaxy that itself sails through an endlessly expanding spatial sea.

Threads of earthlight, moonlight, and starlight weave the finely textured fabric of this galactic arm, interwoven here and there with tracings of another and eternal light, trails of a Presence passing, drawing with them into the future, the beauty, the majesty, the pageantry of unfolding Creation. We feel in this fabric, in the passage of these millennia, the steady splashing of waves, the pulse of rising tides and tides withdrawn.

The tides of time that ripple through the intergalactic ocean of space were not invented by the Maya, who merely observed, noted, and recorded them. As our present wave of consciousness washes highest upon the shore of this world toward the winter solstice of the year A.D. 2011, a Great Cycle

47

(composed of many 5,125-year cycles) will culminate. The new season that dawns then as the days of the southern latitudes shorten and the northern pole moves toward its months of sunlight will be more than the season of a single year.

One knows in advance the hour when the moon will be full. But no one can anticipate the pattern of clouds on the hour of that day, the nature of the jet stream, how the wind may be tossing the waves, at just what moment the moon will break through the clouds, or just what the moonlight will reveal.

These dates foretold by the inhabitants of the Yucatan some twenty-five centuries ago do not speak of how you, in human form, will deal with the new energies that are even now engulfing your world. They speak rather of the time when this earth and the star systems through which she makes her spiral dance will move together into a new galactic field, a field that like a beam radiates forth from the center of this universal envelope. As your solar system moves into this new field of space, the channel that allows the Creator's awareness to reach you comes into perfect alignment.

A moment is coming after which nothing will ever again be thought of as it was before, a metahistorical moment, an event simultaneously alpha and omega to your species and to all your species has ever known.

Here will begin a new season of the universe, for the tide, which only turns with the culmination of *many Great Cycles,* will turn then to begin its slow and patient return to the eternal sea where all awareness *is*—before branching into these streams, these harmonies that coalesce the worlds.

Our race of angelic messengers was ordained at the inception of the human project to awaken you when the time was right. Some of us awaken you from the outside, shaking you and reminding you of who you are. Some of us slide down into physicality, merging our biogravitational fields with yours, awakening within you, looking through your eyes, helping you to reprioritize your lives along the creative currents of love.

Still others of our more distant kin assist entirely from the outside by pouring into the fields of thought and emotion around the earth powerful energies of love, joy, and well-being. These are the spirits who will never incarnate in human form, those of truly extraterrestrial designation. They are not associated with biological processes and never will be. Yet for love of the Great Being who awakens within you, they come to this world as forces of stabilization, beacons of tranquillity, to radiate peace and assurance into this sphere during your decades of awakening.

Throughout these decades, those of us in all three capacities continuously wash the slumbering facets of human thought with the purifying currents of life information. We vitalize you with the renewing energies of eternal love. We help you to roll away the stony conceptions that have prevented the springs of perennial wisdom from bubbling up within you.

It has taken those of us in our particular Light Circle many human walks upon the earth to learn your languages and to familiarize ourselves with your terrestrial imagery. But as we have needed this time to discover the most effective means of reaching through to you with reminders of your purpose, your cultures have needed this time to expand their understanding of reality. And you too have needed this time to reclaim enough of your native intelligence to understand our communications. Cultural understanding remains minuscule in real terms, but at least now it acknowledges the universal context in which your race exists.

Throughout its history your race has labored under successive brands of illusion born of isolated egoic thought. Since these illusions were linguistically enforced in reality descriptions that had no room for our awareness—descriptions that denied our very existence—there were few occasions when our educational currents permitted direct communication with individuals. Since so few had the ability to perceive us, for thousands of years our only means of communication with the *totality of your incarnate being* was to speak to the human races and nations *through their historical processes*. We focused on the gradual development of collective human values, working always to shift human interest from fear-centered thought and activity to thought and activity centered in love.

Twenty thousand years ago we began a cycle of education centered around the spirits of trees and animals. As successive waves of reinforcement came to help us from throughout the galaxies, we were gradually able to attempt more.

Ten thousand years ago, we initiated a higher cycle of education based on the mystery of the seed, the fertility of beasts, and the cycles of the moon. As our reinforcements came at increasingly frequent intervals, we worked together to improve our approach and to introduce as much awareness into human thought as your respective cultures could accommodate. Some five centuries before Christ another wave of us came and found a society in the Yucatan that was—at least at first—most responsive. In the eighteenth century another wave of us came, and this time, thanks largely to the printing press, we were able to stabilize certain insights in human awareness, insights that furthered the decline of aristocracies and revealed the principles of matter and energy that led to the Industrial Revolution.

In 1860 another wave of us came in consciousness to initiate vision in the oppressors and to kindle passions for freedom, justice, and equality in the oppressed. We came then as we come now, into the fields of human consciousness, riding upon the clouds—thought clouds, energy clouds, clouds of awareness—to influence human thinkers and seers, visionaries and poets, leaders, men and women who had not abandoned their love.

In 1900 another wave of us came. In 1914 another. In 1929 yet another. Each time the changes we introduced were dramatic, decisive. Still, errors in judgment were made. Despite the best of our intentions, much of the change occurred too quickly. We determined in the future to allow more time for human adjustment and adaptation.

We were given that time. When several waves of arriving spirit beings converged in the late 1940s, the influx of new consciousness into this earth system encountered—thanks to the success of those who had come before—a new and unprecedented buoyancy of the human spirit. For the first time the power of arriving consciousness was matched with an equal level of human receptivity. We found open a window of opportunity, and it was open wide enough for many of us to slip in, securing places among the new generation.

Though most who found such places were children still, the 1957–1959 awareness wave of this curious and uniquely global generation was bubbling up sufficiently beneath the surface of established human assumptions to suggest to others, older and wiser, that perhaps the gravitational hold of this planet was, after all, negotiable. Change accelerated and accelerated again.

Between the years 1967 and 1969, conceptual communication with incarnate human beings was possible on a large scale for the first time since the fall itself. The first in this present series of conceptual transmissions occurred then. All around the periphery of historical power the consciousness of the world began to change rapidly, but the center of old-world power still held. International bankers, multinational corporate executives, and leaders of governments and world religions were still surrounded with ego defense mechanisms impervious to our awareness.

A decade passed while awareness spread and deepened, working its way like ivy into every crevice of the old, divisive walls. It became more difficult for corruption and deceit to enjoy its former levels of anonymity.

By the late 1970s, when the second in this present series of conceptual transmissions occurred, the new awareness was finding expression in a virtual explosion of new and revolutionary books. The influx of something unprecedented could no longer be denied.

While the growth therapies and the human potential movement caught the currents of new awareness and dressed them in the clothing of the future, the fundamentalist churches caught the same currents and dressed them in the clothing of the past.

But the incoming waves of consciousness still had to penetrate the old bastions of power. These, it was prophesied, would not fall until the more powerful revelations of the late 1980s. By then, *The Starseed Transmissions* noted, the first contractions of planetary birth would be unmistakable.

The Winds of Change

This wave of the late 1980s is the most powerful pulsation of awareness to enter the conceptual atmosphere of human consciousness since before recorded history. And this wave, though it crested during the years 1987 to 1989, has much to yet engulf and utterly change before it has washed fully across the shores of human affairs. The greatest effects of this wave, far surpassing the events of 1987–1989, will come during the late 1990s and the first decade of the twenty-first century.

Like the 1967–1969 period of rapid change, the 1987–1989 intensification of new consciousness has altered the world forever, but unlike that of the 1960s, this change runs deeper; it includes more than just the young, and it extends beyond the visionaries. It has reached deep into the ruling consciousness behind human affairs, injected new thought, new blood, new visions. It has taken root in new people.

High upon a hill in Czechoslovakia, where yesterday stood a statue of Joseph Stalin, a replica of the Liberty Bell now rings out to celebrate democracy and to welcome in a new era of freedom. In Poland elections bring in a new government of the people. Hungarians for the first time see inside the halls of their government as the television lens brings their leaders into their awareness and new awareness to their leaders.

The winds of 1987 to 1989 have inspired the first global reductions in conventional and nuclear weapons. They have eroded the wall that once divided Europe and Berlin and have made possible the spiritual and political reunification of Germany. They have warmed human hearts, made friends of former foes, and melted the icy rigidity that once ruled from the darkened places. They have brought radio, television, and the warmth of new awareness into the heart of yesterday's institutions, thawing the hardness of decades.

The winds of change have brought freedom to millions who had forgotten how to dream. They have warmed the seeds of forgotten hopes long neglected beneath the frozen fields of fear, causing them to sprout and reach toward heaven again. They have taken men from prison and placed them at the helms of nations; they have terminated forever the cold war.

In Japan, and in the nations that border the great Pacific, economic strength has grown beyond what anyone thought possible, bringing with it a new and promising assurance. But though the material progress of the Pacific Rim since World War II has been vast, a deeper and more important progress shows in the happiness of the people, in their heightened enthusiasm for life, in the sparkling eyes of the young. Compare what you see in their eyes today to the eyes of people in movies and photographs of a half century or a century ago.

We who have long been working to change the assumptions beneath the fabric of human life assure you that your world is rapidly being ushered into a new and long-anticipated order. It is not yet without areas of conflict but, with few exceptions, these conflicts are themselves aspects of planetary healing. Hierarchic dominance is everywhere being challenged to release its hold so that new and more democratic societies may be given birth.

These communications of the late 1980s are having a broader and more inclusive effect than our communications of former times. They are not taking place through transmissions or channelings as much as through actual blendings, landings—what shall we call them?—*incarnations*, when our consciousness is able to enter human awareness not just long enough to communicate a message but long enough to remain and stabilize in those who receive the message. These are the Awakened Ones, appearing in every village, every marketplace, every university, every community and city on earth. We are the Creator's agents of decision. The lightning from heaven to earth flows through our consciousness, telepathically connecting us in currents of natural synchronistic action.

The beam of energy information that shines through the center of each of our spirit identities into our respective individualized human lives is the same information beam that emanates from the center of the sun and, before that, from the center of the galactic core. Our essential spirit identity is one with our Creator, the unnameable, the Source who sends but one primal identity beam through galaxy, star, world, and soul, differentiating like light through crystal layers as it flows, taking ever more specific, focused form, yet remaining one light in essence, originating in one Source, one God, one Creator.

We come from the stars, knowing within us the wisdom of stars, knowing the source of every star.

Aligned with our innermost sense of self, flowing uniquely into our spirit lives, the *Eternal Self* individualizes. We come as a family of luminous beings, as a tribe, a light tribe. We come, awakening now in increasing numbers throughout the gentle ones, the lovers of this earth. Those in whom we awaken understand these things in terms quite different from those whom we are still courting from afar. They feel in their bones the changing of the age. And they know that it is good.

As this current wave of consciousness slowly fills the conceptual atmosphere of this planet, more and more people look up from their affairs to notice that their society's understanding of the world is neither complete nor accurate. There are some who shrink away from this truth, but properly understood it is a source of joy and not of fear. The perspective to which we call is one of wholeness. It is the vision that sees, behind the changes of these times, an Eternal Presence slowly filling the fields of human consciousness, a holy Presence, the Presence that inspires life itself.

Those who embrace this vision are both more comfortable and more effective in the arenas where human goods, services, and ideas are exchanged. Their lives are rooted in a sense of peace that weathers well the temporal storms. They use their skills and their insight to prepare the way for change in commercial and political spheres. And as this magical quarter century continues to unfold, their peace continues to deepen. How could it be otherwise? They bring peace to all they encounter.

We address those locked in historical perspectives as best we can, transmitting our information through those of resonant transduction in whom we are able to incarnate occasionally, not necessarily full-time, but long enough to create a work of art, a song, a motion picture, an article, a documentary. As electronic communication devices help to alert more people to the deeper currents of perception within themselves, our transmission of higher-frequency consciousness increasingly takes the form of radiant light energy beamed directly into human awareness. People turn again to the historically neglected flow of information through collective human consciousness, even as that flow is itself being amplified, even as its warmer, love-centered informational currents infiltrate the cooler currents of compartmentalized egoic thought.

From the clouds, the clouds on which some will perceive Christ riding, insight falls like spring rain upon a winter landscape, melting the snows, the prejudice, the illusions of centuries, gathering all in the water of truth and flowing on to warm the currents of a historical river where remnants of ideology bob, like blocks of ice, grinding against one another in the flow, melting subtly, then suddenly, away.

The warm rains of new thought fall steadily upon the fields of human consciousness, bringing warmth, light, and radiant energy. Awakening individual droplets appear from everywhere, it seems, to form powerful new currents, new rivers, new streams. As more people attune to the higher frequencies of awareness, the current swells and flows. New thought, new vision, new perspectives are shared and actualized. Waters—and spirits—rise.

An Information Age is released upon the world, but not before its industrial underpinnings magnify human blind spots and give to humankind unprecedented options—and unprecedented power. Problems intensify. Authoritarian control crumbles. Democracy glows like a morning star. Literacy explodes in the growing light.

Communication technology proliferates, stimulating, awakening, reaching deep into currents and undercurrents of human thought where but a moment ago perception was clouded and curtailed. At first there is little conscious awareness of what is occurring, but there is an inexplicable feeling, a subliminal sense of something wonderful bubbling beneath the crust of culturally enforced perception.

Some associate this with a vague conception of God, but few suspect the immensity of the event that is before them as this new consciousness—aware, alert, active—flows like a tide into the very core of their societies, into their very minds and hearts.

The majority of human beings have not yet thought of reality in broad enough terms to see what is happening. Their belief systems are too constricted; they allow no breadth, no scope, no room for comprehension. They find the evidence of history's direction and gathering momentum too overwhelming to consider.

The possibility that human history may be reaching a climax, a completion, a moment of fulfillment has occurred to only a few. That all that has gone before might be merely the gestational cycle of a developing planetary intelligence is too large a concept, too broad a vision for those cloaked in cultural bias to see.

However, a rapidly growing minority—with significant global influence—has sensed that there is more to current political and economic trends than is typically acknowledged by the world's societies.

These people have seen flickering movements on the other side of the linguistic curtain that hangs between them and a clear view of reality. They have begun to attune to inner levels of being. These awakening individuals are not centered in any one city or nation. They do not belong to any one race or denomination. Without any linear, superficial organization they are looking up and noticing, appearing, incarnating *wherever people love*.

Often the initial phase of their awakening is more emotional than conceptual, but that is enough to allow the coordinated thought and sensation of unified Being to flow into them and their decision making. They may not fully understand it mentally, but they feel something, experience something. They have tapped into a new way of being, they act on it, they trust it. And it works.

There are many individuals now entering positions of global influence who are doing so because they have sensed—often without complete conceptual understanding—that the old ways of consuming information are neither working nor necessary, that there are new and more effective methods of intuitively tapping into living reservoirs of pure information, and they are acting on intuition rather than programming.

These people—without any unifying ideology—are finding themselves in strategic positions overseeing primary systems of planetary energy exchange and human social organization. This is not accidental. When the moment of quantum awakening arrives (or shortly before) they will be guided from within to act in ways that will minimize disruption of the systems that provide human populations with life's necessities.

Before the moment of collective awakening, they will receive full understanding. They will know themselves as cells, terminals—there is not yet an adequate term—biologically incarnate focal points of the same awareness that brings them and their species to life.

Throughout more generations of your ancestors than you are able to remember, informational beings of the angelic orders have been moving within historical circuits, guiding the development of your cultures and your institutions. They have been influencing the evolution of your civilizational deities, filters, and prejudices, so that one day these deities, filters, and prejudices themselves would convince you to look above them, beyond them, into Reality.

Our Educational Goals

Since some three thousand years before the birth of Christ, the most effective components of our educational strategy have been avenues of communication related to sports, agriculture, and music. Recently physics, electronics, and other contemporary fields have also entered the picture. However, regardless of the language we speak—and each of these fields provides us with a language of sorts—our educational goals remain the same.

Our task is to demonstrate the superiority of present-moment, life-centered awareness over awareness clouded by fear. We work to shift human interest gradually away from defensive, survival-oriented lifestyles and toward the pursuit of excellence. We are only able to influence people in areas where their hearts are at least somewhat open and where a passionate interest is present.

We are not interested in changing minds. Minds have always followed the passions of the heart. We are interested in opening hearts.

Our educational vehicles must contrast the advantages of love-centered living with the mediocrity of mere survival, which is the best that fear-centered living claims to offer. They must graphically demonstrate the benefits of the motivation of love as opposed to the motivation of fear, illustrating the superiority of cooperation over conflict, negotiation over confrontation, forgiveness over revenge, present-moment awareness over perception filtered through the past. They must show these as superior methods of achieving human goals and interests.

Since the day when we first challenged Sumerian warriors to see who could hurl their spears the farthest—instead of hurling them at each other—we have utilized the vehicle of sports to harness the currents of human aggression and channel them into more creative activity. As human aggression is channeled into athletic competition, a subtle shift in values occurs. In many cultures it has taken generations for this shift to produce new patterns of accepted social behavior, but ultimately the shift does come.

In this century the most significant transformations in human consciousness have occurred on the playing fields of the world, in stadiums and swimming pools, on basketball courts and skating rinks, in streets, back lots, and alleyways. Here the majority of human beings first encounter their instinctual natures.

Wherever human aggression can be released upon the playing field, channeled into a game of competition where skills are pitted against skills and where all abide by commonly agreed-upon rules, the collective reservoir of human emotional energy releases the pent-up steam of potential violence and *that particular tendency toward violence is removed from circulation.*

The transmutation of aggressive energy is one of several functions served by physical sports. Another is to agree upon rules that are in the mutual interests of two opposing sides or teams, rules that are to everyone's advantage to learn and obey—a basic lesson perhaps, but a significant watershed in each individual's cycle of awakening. Team sports go beyond individual sports by encouraging players to think first of the team (the greater whole) and to help other players succeed. They call upon athletes to perfect the physical capabilities of the human body and to help others do the same. Some sports do more than merely transmute aggression. Baseball offers a state-of-the-art educational context. On the diamond historical blind spots are penalized, while the psychological and emotional skills essential to a universal species are rewarded.

Those of us who are guiding humankind through the educational processes that precede awakening do occasionally channel our energy through the structures of organized religion when the motives of those involved originate in love and their intentions are for the common good. But Fatimas and Ballinaspittles are few and far between; they are the exceptions, not the rule. Despite the best of intentions, attempts to organize spirituality almost always fall back upon themselves, masking the spirit and occasionally even flipping over to become the embodiment of whatever they oppose.

By their nature spiritual organizations are superfluous. They seek to do what is already done. A successful church is transitional, a stepping-stone toward consciousness, not a rock upon which generations duplicate the mistakes of the past.

To orient your life around a structure of some other human being's understanding is to worship a false god. It is to lock yourself into a framework of someone else's prejudice, however well intentioned. It is to prefer the past-oriented knowledge of another to your own present-moment perception. It is to doubt both yourself and the Creator who would, if you permit it, awaken within you. So it has been written, "They stand in God's Presence yet see only their idols. Their eyes look upon images of beauty engraved in stone and in the faces of coins, yet do not see the living beauty all around them."

Those who orient their lives around human organizations are left with little happiness and less satisfaction. They are like mice on a treadmill of self-validating and self-defeating beliefs. Until they choose to step off the treadmill, there is little we can do to reach them. For they alone have the right to determine how they will understand themselves and their world, and they have the freedom to maintain the world they have chosen, however limiting.

We can only shepherd such people from afar, as we have shepherded human beings throughout history, breaking up their routines when appropriate, to give them opportunities to look at the world from larger perspectives. But we cannot compel change.

No lasting change is ever wrought from without.

These days we find a few individuals in every community who begin to suspect that there might be something beyond their culture's understanding of reality. When this occurs, we have a breakthrough, a beachhead. These we can and do reach. Generally, it is then only a short time before these first-to-awaken translate their new awareness into terms better suited than ours to convey it to others locked within their particular brand of illusion, thereby helping to awaken them also.

In historical societies this is the prime function of art. As artistic insight gradually sifts down through the numerous layers of tradition, its essence at last reaches the level of politics. Then transformation happens rapidly—at times too rapidly. You saw something of this process at work during the American, French, and Russian revolutions. With too few Awakened Ones consciously involved in the process, we succeeded in lighting the fires of love for freedom, but we failed to control the flames.

There are always random factors in any social upheaval, the degree of uncertainty increasing in proportion to the rate and extent of change. Disruption is not always negative. A day provides a welcome disruption of night. A star disrupts the surfaces of nearby worlds. Biological life disrupts the otherwise steady slumber of inorganic molecules.

As clear currents of higher awareness flow ever more freely among human thought, the murky biases of yesterday are disrupted, loosened, and washed away. Introduce these currents we must, but always our goal is to do so as gently as possible. We release the energy of new awareness into spheres of human tradition where it is vital, but people alone—and the choices they make in their moments and hours—can determine whether the resulting transformations are graceful or traumatic.

The currents of thought we bring are no more stationary than the sap of a living tree in the midsummer sun, or the pulse of a being in love. The words that have been assigned to our thought currents today may appear in printed pages tomorrow as triggers, memory catalysts, or sparks to ignite and renew awareness, but words are not truth. Truth is eternal; its verbal representations are not. They live and grow and change like the herbs and grasses along the banks of a stream, like the water flowing by.

The perspectives we share in these transmissions are formulations of an eternal stream of consciousness. They are meaningful for a moment, perhaps for a day. They provide a place of understanding where you can rest as you move forward on your homeward journey. They are stepping-stones appearing before you to take you across the stream of consciousness, from the subconscious shore where you have floundered in the marshes and swamplands of history to the conscious shore where you are aware of the singularity of consciousness you knew when the world was young.

As you move across the stream, you notice something strange and beautiful: each new gain in comprehension brings a corresponding reduction of complexity. You become simpler as you become wiser, until the day arrives when

once again your understanding is your own, no longer polluted with what you have been told or what you have heard,
but fresh as new perception, pure as a mountain spring,
clear as the guileless eyes of a conscious child.

7

The Spontaneous Precision of Instinct

*A*s every good athlete and martial artist knows, there is an intuitive, natural way of being that is essential to swift and effective response to the rapid shift of energies and opportunities inherent in each moment. One cannot play a good game of tennis while making rational decisions on how to proceed. A shortstop does not make a leaping catch, twirl 180 degrees while still in the air, and fire the ball to second base for the double play by pursuing an analytical process and mentally deciding how to proceed. The home-run hitter does not connect with a 95-mph pitch by consciously analyzing the trajectory and velocity of the ball and calculating where to place the bat.

A process of reasoning does in fact occur in each of these instances, but it is a superior form of reasoning that occurs below the level of the athlete's conscious awareness, with speed and accuracy surpassing that of even the most advanced computers. Athletes who reach excellence in their chosen sport have learned to trust a type of rational analysis that occurs almost instantaneously below the level of typical, historical thought.

In the coming age it will be not just athletes and martial artists who experience this but everyone in every field. Before the coming millennium is full, such intuitive response to the moment will be taken for granted. It will become a matter of course. This divine dance of inner direction is humankind's natural way of being.

There are times when it is appropriate for decision making to be slowed to a mental level, but what was intended *to be chosen consciously* as an occasional option has become the historical norm. It has become the typical way historical peoples have determined their lives. In fact, human beings were never driven from any primordial paradise. Their decision to place exclusive emphasis on the cumbersome rational thought processes of their egos and to ignore, and eventually forget, their intuitive ways of processing information altered their perceptual apparatus to such an extent that they could no longer see the beauty and wonder of the earth around them.

The information that enters your awareness is subject to interpretation by two separate yet potentially (and prehistorically) compatible systems. The system designed to be your primary system functions autonomically below the level of conscious awareness. In that system information is organized and interpreted by the spirit. In the system designed initially to be your backup or supplemental system, information is organized and interpreted by subjective associations. This system, of course, is the one with which you are historically most familiar.

The Ego and the Spirit

Decision making for the eternal spirits who chose to inhabit human biology was never intended to be dominated by sensory input. In healthy function the incarnate being receives the body's sensory input only after it is distilled by the computerlike circuitry of the spirit's primary informational system. In the right hemisphere of the brain, sensory information is processed instantaneously, the pertinent essence being immediately projected upon the awareness screen of the resident spirit.

The body-associated sense of self or ego shares this same biocircuitry. When the ego functions in a healthy, symbiotic relationship with the resident spirit, whose reflection it is, it has no need to think its way through the meaning of each and every sensory signal.

During the early incarnations, when the first wave of spirits entered human form, the importance of the ego was not yet fully understood. Experience quickly showed that without an aspect of identity specializing in the material plane and the requirements of the body, one of two things was likely to happen: Either the ultraconscious spirit, relatively insensitive to the frequencies of fear, would carelessly damage or destroy the body through some oversight—often as simple as forgetting it was incarnate—or, at the other extreme, the spirit would become so preoccupied with the unfamiliar nuances of material biology that its consciousness would no longer be free for the creative and interpretative enjoyments that were its fundamental reasons for projecting the body in the first place.

The solution, of course, was to designate a portion of awareness as a resident material plane expert, one who fully understood not merely the necessity of fear, for the angels understood that much, but also the mechanics of how fear worked. This portion of awareness (ego) would then prioritize and regulate the currents of fear that would inevitably be a part of any excursion into the realms of matter, when necessary calling the resident spirit back from the brink of behavior likely to prove biologically damaging.

So it was that ego and spirit, two facets of a whole, divided responsibilities between them and shared the same human body. In healthy function their symbiotic collaboration is as closely woven as the twin threads of the DNA spiral. In the expression of the first incarnate ones, spirit and ego were so entwined that in any moment the distinction itself could not be made. Like alternating current, their awareness patterns oscillated in a configuration of perfect harmony. The ego knew it was a facet of the spirit, and therefore it shared the spirit's joy, enthusiasm, and understanding. The only times when the ego might become distinct—and such times did occur occasionally—were when the attention of the incarnate one became so preoccupied that the incarnate one neglected sensory input of major importance.

When immersed in exciting creative projects, spirits often orient their informational sensors selectively, filtering out some of their input in order to devote more of their attention to the project. In these cases the ego broke in when needed. Its interruptions were not always dramatic; often it would merely remind the spirit that its body required water, food, or rest.

While the spirit would dispassionately review sensory input with the clear-sighted objectivity of eternal awareness, the ego, on the other hand, proceeded differently. Its way of utilizing and experiencing the branching, treelike human nervous system was unlike the spirit's. The ego *feels* the human nervous system subjectively, sensuously, slowly, and in detail, taking time to groom and care for the body and attend to its needs. Though different, the ego's and the spirit's respective uses of the human nervous system were both vital, both essential to a balanced incarnate experience.

When the fall occurred, the entire human determination of "good and evil" shifted over to the ego's slower and more cumbersome manner of interpreting/digesting/eating the sensory input of the human nervous system. This slow, cumbersome, rational analysis of sensation played a necessary role in the ego's designated range of responsibility, but by its very nature it was subjective. Guided and directed by the spirit, the ego provided a valuable investigative tool for in-depth studies of a material nature. However, without the overview of the spirit it became truly myopic. By nature, the ego's view of itself and its surroundings was partial and incomplete. Its slower but highly specified left-brain analysis of sensory information was a powerful and—even after the fall—fully operational vehicle for terrestrial research and development. Yet without the spirit's direction, it made no difference how well the left-brain process operated. The mind was like a high-powered vehicle driven blindly.

A lonely ego, defining itself in mortality and isolation, lacks the scope and expansiveness of the spirit. When it single-handedly attempts to operate a human mind, it is like a toddler wearing the oversized garments of an adult. It feels smothered beneath something made for another and larger being. It does not have the energy needed to use such an exquisite biological tool. Without the spirit, the ego is capable of using only about 10 percent of the brain's capacity, and even then its observations and conclusions are often inaccurate.

A mind that conceives of itself as fundamentally separate from all that it perceives is an instrument of division. It can do nothing but divide, analyze, compartmentalize, and dissect. Everything on which it turns its attention is reduced to disconnected segments, while the spirit, the life of the whole, is forgotten. With the fictitious premise that it is fundamentally distinct from both God and nature lying at the root of its thinking, it is not capable of reason, for its premise is a lie.

This is why the historical egoic use of the human mind has been so destructive: it creates thoughts, images, personal identity structures, cultural institutions, *and ultimately entire civilizations* that are based upon the illusion that the individual is fundamentally distinct from the ground of being from which it and all creation have emerged.

Only the spirit has the necessary energy, intelligence, and operational software to use the full capacity of the human mind. When the awareness of spirit fills a human mind, it is an instrument of unity, an instrument of harmony, an instrument of cooperation, creation, understanding. It becomes a transformational vortex, a channel through which universal awareness can flow into this physical world.

As a component in the spiritual structure of the universal intelligence flowing through humankind into the earth, egoic thought has a valued place, but when functioning in isolation without the overview of the spirit, its reasoning, prone as it is to fearful exaggeration, creates chaos, disorder, and disease. Perceiving separation where none exists, imagining itself, its species, the plants, animals, even the world itself as existing in fundamental distinction, egoic thought separated from spirit is devastating to people, to the environment, and to the other life-forms who share that environment.

The decision making resulting from human reliance on exclusively egoic thought has given ample evidence of its inadequacy during these past millennia. Yet until now there was no other way. The voluntary cooperation of human egos could not be coerced. It has required this cycle of historical education to bring your race to its current level of consciousness and egoic receptivity, when at last we can communicate clearly with you.

Even now your spirit-directed biocircuitry is processing information outside the range of your conscious awareness, outlining your behavioral options and determining which among them represent your most creative pattern of interaction. If these intuitive processes were slowed and explained, if the many factors of which your ego is not aware were outlined and their multiple implications shown, your ego would find nothing beyond its comprehension.

The basic building blocks of instinctual logic are the same as those used by the ego's slower reason, differing only in speed and accuracy. Yet to access the deep intuitive wisdom of the life force, one cannot demand such explanation or interrupt the flow of moments by insisting upon a step-by-step breakdown of the spirit's subliminal analysis. One must simply trust and observe the results.

Spontaneity is a rational process in the constitution of love. Its accuracy is unsurpassed. It is not clouded by fear-rooted emotions, cultural bias, or addiction to linguistically structured thought.

The nonresistant superconductivity of inner biological computing organizes data at the speed of light—and with a clarity that complements the purposes of the Children of the Light.

Living Instinctually

In the historical condition, instinctual input is ignored.

The cultures that dominate human values mistrust it so deeply, in fact, that children are taught from their earliest years to fear their instincts. Young people intuitively sense that without help their egos are incapable of effectively managing their affairs, and culture plays upon this sense. It distorts the truth behind this insight by teaching each new generation that since their egos are inadequate, they must develop a social persona, a protective veneer, an image of themselves behind which they can then retreat in safety, forever after pursuing physical-plane relationships from behind a mask.

Occasionally overtly, but more often through a thousand forms of subliminal persuasion issuing from virtually every culturally adjusted person they encounter, the young are taught that the development of a self-image is an urgent matter of grave importance.

The sense of self that culture's children subsequently adapt is superficial and fictitious. If their former self-awareness was inadequate, they are certain that this new substitute is even more so. And so they begin their outward orientation, looking always to others—parents, teachers, authority figures—for guidance, direction, and understanding of reality. Often they stay in such outward orientation for the rest of their lives, assigning so little value to the inner voice of the spirit that soon their instincts atrophy, all but forgotten. Like the others in their sleepwalking society, they begin calculating their life values, using the ego's unwieldy and often anxiety-permeated processes of reasoning. Their skill at this is the only measure of success they are taught to value.

To live spontaneously, instinctually. To simply be. To say the right words without thinking them out ahead of time. To experience the purity of a mind uncluttered by troublesome and misplaced responsibility. To know exactly the right gesture, the right behavior, the creative response for each and every situation. Such are the birthrights of each and every human being.

Every child comes into the world with his or her instinctual awareness healthy and intact. In the coming civilizations of the stars, children will mature not only retaining this ability but developing it, honing it to a fine art. They and their societies will live instinctually from moment to moment, as you are now invited to begin living. Trust yourself, your instincts, your intuitive senses. Accept the birthright that has unfolded with you from out of the Being behind all being.

Human design has emerged from the highest currents of a supreme intelligence. It is worthy of your trust.

You have been conditioned to fear what you might do if you were to act spontaneously, but such fear is based upon a lie. You are not evil at your core, not forged in sin. The universe has created in you not a demon or a fool but a magnificent, luminous being. You share eternity's creative power and all the wondrous beauty of time. You share a single unified field of awareness with angels and with the Star Maker. Should you fear the spontaneity that will reveal your beauty? Should you fear the expression of your love?

To funnel your expression of life through the narrowness of another's anticipated response is the beginning of death. You do so at the cost of your vitality. There is another way. Its essence is trust.

72

Below the level of conscious awareness, feel the informational input of your surroundings flow freely in and out of your soul. Feel it enter deep within you to be processed easily, autonomically, in accordance with life's design. When you relax and release your biology to flow in the uninhibited rhythmic currents of the love that animates all creation, your life force naturally organizes the data that flows through your center of observation. Masterfully, impeccably, it brings into your momentary awareness what is most important to your soul.

Do not sacrifice upon the altar of your mind the sacred wisdom that rises with each beat of your heart. Do not let the grim priests of tradition tear out the very heart of the spontaneous currents that carry the insight of eternity. Let your mind relax in love and openness until it becomes an altar upon which the Creator's consciousness descends. Spring bareback upon the naked energy of life and ride its current into your decisions. The inherent intelligence of life itself will bring you understanding of self and world and guide you unerringly into the future.

It is far better to have a poor self-image than an image crafted in conceit. When the winds of change grow too strong for the fictions of humans—as soon they will—those with a poor self-image will let it go and find themselves in God. But those who already are full of themselves have no room for God, and they will resist any change that threatens the illusion they have worked so long to establish.

When you receive God, you receive the consciousness that precedes all manifestation, the limitless consciousness of eternal love that was from the beginning, is now, and ever shall be—before, beyond, above, and within all relationship. This consciousness is the greatest gift that anyone could ever receive.

As you allow your life to be guided by the currents of indigenous wisdom flowing instinctually from within, you receive this gift, you find yourself immersed in the animating emanations of the universe. Upon the frequencies of eternal love you rediscover your purpose. You remember your reason for this lifetime's incarnation, for taking on human form. You discover that you have access to an ocean of living information. Your access code is a child's trust.

8

This Season's Children

Yours is the story of a flower pushing its way gradually upward through the snows of materialism until finally it breaks through the surface crust of rigid tradition and emerges into the light of a new season. It has been hard for you of individual consciousness during this human winter, but you come from hardy stock. And the warming you now feel is no illusion.

You see the sun arch higher in the heavens, higher than it has ever been before. You sense the changes in the air and know an age is turning. The snows of history's many perceptual crystallizations have all but melted away, while beneath them you have been moving ever closer to the light of this new day. What is this tradition of bending low? The snows are neither so heavy nor as lasting as when these cultural habits were fashioned. The age of ice is swiftly passing. You need not live as if you still carried the weight of history, so grave, so serious. Come! Entertain the consciousness of the stars.

Relax your heavy conceptions, the blocks and bricks that form history's icy walls. There are lands outside these walls, beyond these cultural corridors that narrow your awareness of self and world. You see more clearly now than those who formed these solemn views in the coldest hours of the night.

The world has been thawing for some time.

A new awareness crackles behind the eyes of children in Beijing and Adelaide, in Kiev and Tokyo, in Chicago, São Paulo, and Capetown. A new generation of little flowers rises through the melting snows of former centuries. They lift their heads now, like crocuses, tulips, daffodils, blooming to speak to their elders of a better way.

You who are the parents of this new generation, listen to what this season's children have to say. They do not reject you or the principles that have guided your lives. But they know they must *do what you have not yet done.*

Their destiny is to complete the achievement begun.

Be gentle with them, these literal flowers of your love. Do not crush them beneath the ceilings of windowless schools that bury them in facts they cannot understand without the natural light of spirit. Let them move beyond the established corridors of historical ways, into the sunlight and open air of new meaning and new experience. Use your centers of learning, your school systems, to assist them in doing what no human generation has ever before done: Help them to blossom into all they can be—sure of themselves, confident in the wisdom, the life that lives within them.

Give your children the tools of your culture as you would give paint and canvas to an artist. But do not tell them what to draw. Help them learn to express themselves in terms meaningful to them and to those in the world around them. Offer them skills to help express themselves more fully. The self this generation expresses in uninhibited creativity is the Great Self, which seeks birth into your world.

As you help your children to better express themselves, do not make them feel that they are incomplete without your training, that they are partial beings in need of years of academic processing to be whole or satisfied with themselves. If you give them this impression, you make them cripples, with a vested interest in those very illusory self-images that are even now melting in the warmer winds of love's approaching season. Help your children; do not handicap them and make it more difficult for them to adapt to these times of accelerating change.

These next two decades will see the most rapid period of change any human civilization has ever known. To ride the currents of that great change, young and old alike will require all their native wit and sensibilities.

If you care about the young people who will reach adulthood in the 1990s and in the first decade of the twenty-first century—the children who are in your schools today—share with them all the knowledge you will, but preserve their inherent confidence in themselves, for this is how they show their confidence in God.

A child's level of confidence is a major factor in determining his or her future success. The preservation of a child's native esteem is far more important than the acquisition of technical skills. Many of these little ones have not forgotten the Great Being who shines through the filter of their individuality. Your role is to help them grow in such a way that they do not forget. Assist the incarnation of the eternal spirits who dance above their lives.

When you see first their beauty and perfection, when you affirm their eternal reality of being, when you see it in their eyes, you cannot help but draw it forth. Bring out the best in them and in all whom you encounter. Give no energy to the fictions of those who do not know their immortality, but see instead the spirit who seeks to incarnate there, within that individuality. Acknowledge that Being. Relate to it. Draw it forth. Help another dimension of eternity slip quietly into your times. Help this new generation to awaken.

And you, of younger years—you will not make the people around you happy doing what you think they want you to do.

Only through being yourself can you give to the others in your world your greatest gifts. To do any less betrays both them and yourself.

There are many people who, decades after adolescence, continue to live their lives based on how they think their parents want them to live. It is appropriate to respect parents, to listen to their ideas, suggestions, advice—and there are many instances in which parental input is in harmony with the pursuit of your own purposes, many instances in which it can help you cut through illusion and become more fully yourself. But it is *you* who must evaluate this input; you alone must decide the direction your life is to take. For where do parents stop and where does society begin?

Do not cut yourself off from ideas and suggestions that come from those whom you admire and respect. Listen to others with all your senses, intuiting between their words, feeling the essence of spirit behind what they are expressing, considering their input. But ultimately, you must decide in your own heart, and there alone. Base *your* decisions on *your* perception. To inhabit the new awareness, you are required to be yourself, for when you are, you are a beautiful being, in touch with your eternal dimension, conscious of the generations that will follow you, conscious of generations that came before, immersed in the love that lights and unites the leaves of all generations upon life's singular tree.

In the fields of thought that surround this planetary sphere, for those with ears to hear, radiates the essential wisdom of the wisest of those who have gone before. In these fields there is a message circulating from the elders of your species tree, a message intended for your global village of today. If it could be clothed in words, what the grandparents, the ancestors say, it would be something like this:

> Do what we have always dreamed of doing but did not quite achieve. You do not know, young ones, what we had to work against and how much easier we have made it for you. We feel as though we have almost done it. Go one step beyond. Do what we have almost done.

Create a world where our descendants will not have to struggle and fight as we have struggled, as we have fought—a cooperative world, a peace-filled world. Create it first in your hearts and homes. In our time this was our challenge. In your time it is yours. You see how well we met this task, this challenge. We have done better than some perhaps and not as well as others, but it is no matter now. You are this season's people.

We speak to you, children of the twentieth century: Do not throw away your caution. Do not open yourselves to those who would exploit you or deprive you of your rights. But please, live with less fear than we did. The rights you enjoy today are here to stay. Armed struggle is not essential to the procurement of your daily bread. This much we have given you. There are still those who would take advantage of you, but they are fewer and less powerful than they were in our time. The communication tools you have today make it far more difficult for those who would abuse power. Perhaps the most important lesson our lives have taught us is this:

You are always better off communicating, with friends, with enemies—it makes no difference. Be open, honest. State your views as clearly as possible. Do not be afraid of giving away secrets. It is best to have no secrets; they are the source of much mistrust. Share with others who you are, your goals, your ambitions. We have found that on those occasions when we have communicated with our adversaries, miracles have occurred. Across national borders, across racial lines, across economic and social barriers, breakthroughs of understanding have occurred. We came to respect those with whom we spoke and they came to respect us. These are the friendships that have served us well in our lives.

Agreement is less important than respect, for with respect agreement may one day occur, but without it agreement is impossible. Honesty and openness will earn you respect. The times we fought when we did not need to fight, we lost both the fight and potential friends. Count everyone a potential friend, then do what you can to make that friendship real. Communication is a power much greater than confrontation. Do not lose sight of that.

We have seen, as all the elders of our race have seen, that there is no scarcity of resources. The only scarcities have been of love—and of imagination.

As long as the sun shines and rivers flow, as long as the winds blow and ocean waves lap upon these shores, there is no shortage of energy, nor is there anything over which to fight, unless perhaps your basic needs are denied by another's greed. Then we would say, yes, defend your rights, but speak first, communicate first. Use all your wit and ingenuity to avoid the conflict; then, if you must, defend what you must. But know you may well lose as much as you will gain. Use force only in defense and only as a last resort. There is no cause but defense that justifies violence.

No nation whose people are motivated for any reason other than defense can win a war in the present climate of the world.

Perhaps this was not always true. But the wise ones among us have noticed this, and whatever its cause, it is the reality of the times in which you live. Can you understand? This is the real news. Consider what it means. No nation desires to lose a war, and if only a defensive war can be won, who will launch a war? Can nations battle in mutual defense?

If your youth pumps passion through your blood and you desire an arena in which to test your spirit fire, turn to the athletic field, to the Olympic Games, to amateur and professional sports, to baseball, basketball, football, soccer, rugby, hurling, skiing, sailing, bicycling, dancing, cross-country racing. The options before you are endless. Choose the field that best suits your nature. Compete to your heart's content. Enjoy the pursuit of excellence. Compete in marketplaces and music halls, in fields and amphitheaters.

But if you seek to enjoy your lives, do not compete on the battlefield. Leave behind the old world's greatest bane. Do not kill. Do not destroy. Do not maim, murder, and ruin. In the end, you but do these things to yourselves. There are no "others." Let your competition be lighthearted and friendly. Celebrate the diversity of excellence. We have lived that you might know a brighter world. Do not throw away the promise we have given you. If you turn to violence in any of its forms, you betray those of us who have gone before you and those of us who will follow.

There are no winners in violent confrontation, only losers—and more losers.

Do not let the pursuit of excellence in your chosen field blind you to the excellence of another. See the same spirit in them, pursuing the same excellence to which you aspire. Appreciate them in the same way you appreciate the skilled opponent who helps you hone and develop your skills. Appreciate them as you would a partner, a coach, a trainer who helps you transcend what you thought were your limitations.

These attitudes, simple though they are, lie at the heart of the world we want you to know.

9

The Right Use of Language

The term *spelling* is used to describe the mechanics of language. And *spelling*, in the sense of casting or projecting forth a binding illusion, has been the chief activity of historical languages.

Language is the mechanism of matter's spell, the means through which the spell is maintained from one generation to the next. Those who slumber beneath linguistic illusions limit themselves to the deficiencies, blind spots, and biases of a particular method of symbolism, which even at its best can convey no more consciousness than the consciousness of those who invented it. They imagine that without verbal, conceptual understanding there can be no understanding.

Understanding can be symbolized and to some extent conveyed through words, but understanding itself requires language no more than a bird requires a cage. *Understanding comes only through experience.* And for experience, there has never been—and never will be—a substitute.

Instead of serving as a tool of your creative expression to help you sculpt and mold sound and light into forms of beauty and grace, your Babylonian primate tongues have defined you, limited you, and kept you in the narrow definition prisons of the cultures that gave them birth.

Belief systems are illusions of linguistically structured thought. They have been the means through which these guttural languages have limited your perception. They are cages created by words, imprisoning their makers. Even insights that accurately reflect reality cannot be preserved effectively by a belief system.

The very attempt to hold on to the truth destroys its living nature. The same fruit cannot be both growing on the tree and preserved in a jar; it must be one or the other. The garden of living information that surrounds those who open their hearts in love is so prolific, its fruits so abundant, that there is no need for individual, organizational, or cultural preservation.

The universe sustains visions and ideas that are in its interest.

What you struggle to retain is not the truth. The truth is always with you. It could not be otherwise. Some of that truth you feel and recognize. Some may be still hidden from your eyes, to be revealed another day, another hour, when it is needed and not before. The truth that is portrayed in the words of human language is an external symbol of the truth that lives within you. It is an artifact, a key, designed to open the passageway that connects you with the Living Truth. The words that trigger comprehension are no longer important once comprehension is accessed.

Below the level of linguistically centered thought, the life-giving current of truth flows continuously. The purpose of these accompanying words is to keep your mind occupied while these currents bring you a deeper perception.

The phrases we use in these transmissions are designed as closely as possible around the living currents of truth that radiate from the consciousness that is now filling the thought fields of this world. These living currents of truth are preverbal. They are the reality of this communication. These words are but their symbolic representatives.

As you read through these pages, meaning rises gradually beneath the level of your thought. As understanding surfaces from time to time and appears in your awareness, you achieve an insight. Each new insight becomes like a rung on a ladder, allowing the part of you it touches to awaken from the dormancy of ancient conditioning. With each new insight you climb yet another rung, leaving behind another layer of illusion. Upward, away from a matter-bound view of the world, into the sunlit regions you rise, into a world where you know yourself as a reflection of the One who has come to these realms to be, and to be among, the many.

You do not need to study these transmissions, analyzing and categorizing them as human minds have done with our teachings in the past. One who camps upon the rungs of a ladder is as foolish as one who carries it along with him. You have only to allow these thoughts, as you encounter them, to trigger what changes they may in your own field of perception as you continue to move forward. Do not struggle for the kind of understanding that comes through effort. Intellectual effort has a place in mechanical disciplines but not in the reactivation of your spiritual perception, for that comes only when all efforts of the ego have ceased and you accept yourself, ground zero, just as you are. When you relax and accept yourself, comprehension rises unfailingly into your awareness. Like water surfacing in a spring, understanding appears. It seeks the surface of your thoughts. If you do not desensitize this surface with the oily impurities of self-doubt, or seal it off with some crust of ideological ice, understanding will be there for you—a wellspring that will never run dry.

Accept the understanding that emerges in response to the moments of your life. Do not strive for more comprehension than that which appears effortlessly. You will know what you need to know and remember what you have forgotten.

Let these transmissions wash over you like a gentle rain, our words splashing across the surface of your awareness, flowing over all that you are, rinsing away the soil of the night. There is no need to hold these thoughts. Let them flow, and with them will go the soiled stains of misassumption.

The current of insight that flows through this material and into your awareness needs to continue its flow beyond you, outward and away again. It is a passing stream of consciousness, a light current of thought. If you are drawn toward its translation into human media, keep its purpose always in mind: *to rekindle in others awareness of God,* to bring others—by the most direct form of communication available—into awareness of the Eternal Being who lives in their hearts.

The greatest healers who have ever walked this earth were great not because they healed large numbers of people but because they healed the right person, the strategic "other" in their lives who most required their love. If your communication reaches through to but one other person, you have succeeded: The transition to posthistoric times will unfold without trauma, without fear or upheaval, and our goal will be accomplished in full.

The translations of this eternal stream of consciousness into human languages are meant to last for only a short time. They are intermediary sparks to bridge the illusory gap between human hearts and the heart of God.

10

Opening the Etheric Antenna

To the seasoned traveler of the stars, a race who lives daily with access to a universe's library of information without ever making use of it is more primitive than a race who has yet to discover fire. So simple a thing, the discovery of fire, yet so immense, so revolutionary the changes it brings. So simple a thing, the discovery of God . . .

Awakening the sensitivity that allows you to access universal information requires a flip of thinking: it requires that you look from above rather than from below. It requires an accurate knowledge of self. Yet you cannot know yourself until your *images* of self are dissolved, and only love is capable of that dissolution.

Feel love being offered to you from the life that rises in your veins, feel love being offered to you in the sunlight that shines upon your home, in the rains that fall upon the fields that provide your grains, in the eyes of a child, partner, or friend. The love available to you in each moment is more than enough to dissolve the subtle ties that bind you in illusion. You are worthy, you are deserving of that love.

The Process of Awakening

Relaxing again into the fields of pure perception that glow as God's awareness, releasing attachment to human knowledge, both personal and collective, letting go of favored concepts, images, and beliefs—these are steps in a psychological process that each person must move through in the course of awakening.

This process allows your spirit-world sensitivity to blossom. It causes you to understand from a new perspective both your individuality and the whole of which you are a part. It does not destroy or diminish your ego; it merely washes away the illusions that have made your ego miserable. It releases your understanding of self from the bonds of gravity that hold it in struggle and fear.

For if your ego is a reflection of spirit, then even at its core, your ego is spirit. It is distinct from spirit as the image in a mirror is distinct from the object being reflected, but without the one there would not be the other. When the reflective glass of your material biology—and your understanding of it—is clear and clean, both ego and spirit benefit from a world perceived anew.

Your *spirit* draws its first sense of identity from the high-frequency energies of the Constellation of Love. Your *ego* draws its first sense of identity from the slower, materially attractive frequencies in the Constellation of Truth. Yet both constellations exist in the same sea of Eternal Being, and in a healthy state both spirit and ego perform their respective roles equally centered in God.

The psychological process leading to awakening, though it can be described in many ways, is fundamentally a process of identity shift from a linguistically defined sense of self, rooted in your ego and an exaggerated sense of your vulnerability, to a sense of identity rooted in the unified field of consciousness that lies behind and within all individuality. During the process your sense of self blossoms into an accurate awareness of who you are. This transformed awareness includes your former sense of being one among many, but it also includes an awareness of a reality greater than the ever-changing worlds of form, an awareness rooted in the singularity of Eternal Being from which all individuality unfolds.

As you awaken into this awareness, you know yourself simultaneously as *one among many* and as *One at the source of many*. It is impossible to be truly individual without this awareness.

Without this awareness you are a latent possibility, a programmed product of human culture. You are not truly yourself. You are certainly not incarnate in any literal sense of the term. Remember, your choices are always honored. If you prefer an image to reality, the image is what you experience.

The psychological process is an initiation of sorts, a rite of passage. It demonstrates your willingness to turn away from a language-based understanding of reality and to restore your trust in reality itself, in the Eternal Being at the source of your life. It requires courage. You must leap naked into eternity's promise, stripped of the assurances of time, certain only that the vast benevolence that has given birth to this universe is more worthy of trust than the belief-system deities of the historical order.

The psychological process requires courage for another reason as well. To undergo it, you must be willing to accept the wonder, the power, the awesome reality of human design. No belief system requires such responsibility. On the contrary, belief systems offer to assume responsibility for you, protecting you from yourself, sheltering you beneath their many brands of dogmatic illusion. You do not have to face the truth if you hire a belief system to do it in your place. But belief systems demand a stiff price. They place a heavy tax on your energy. They siphon off the better part of your awareness. They confiscate your eternal sense of self and lock you into a flicker of fictitiously described time. Throughout history, humankind has paid this price.

The intensifying frequencies of love now make it easier for people everywhere to see what their saints and visionaries have always seen. Those who receive their impressions with the openness of a child feel an eternal consciousness seeping slowly between their thoughts. As their interest in the superficial chatter of the ego wanes, their attention turns to matters of relevance. They experience a cycle of blending during which they learn to sustain their awareness in the eternal awareness that is growing steadily in the thought fields around the earth. Universal intelligence can then flow freely through them and into expression. Their centers of identity ride the crest of the eternal wave, at the perfect point where One Being spills over into the many beings of time.

As an informational cell in this awakening planetary field, the extent of your consciousness determines your range of mobility. The extent of your consciousness is limited only by your ability to love and to embrace with your love the space around you, and all it contains.

Just as the cells of a human body are woven into the life and consciousness of the body as a whole, so too are love-centered human lives entwined in the life of God.

As you use human circuitry in accordance with its design, as you use it to transform the powerful bioelectric currents of terrestrial energy into cycles of life-enhancing activity on the physical plane, you will come to understand more fully the awesome capacities of the human mind. When *you*—eternal spirit—use your mind to gather and step down the energies of universality, focusing and channeling them into specific dimensional creation, your mind's activity is so different, its capacities enhanced so far beyond its typical historical usage, that one could say with some accuracy that it is not the same mind at all.

In the emerging paradigm of the spirit, conceptual understanding is of secondary consequence; those who function on the frequencies of love do not demand it at every step in their creative processes. Their activity is therefore able to flow freely, rapidly, unhindered by the constant need to tabulate mentally each and every detail. They understand *spiritually* with their hearts and *tangibly* with their bodies. They also understand with their minds, should they choose to slow down enough to access that mental understanding. But—as lovers often do—they frequently choose to forego such a detailed analysis.

Beings who function in a state of grace are secure in the knowledge that conceptual understanding is there whenever they choose to slow into it, but they have released their addiction to the "fruit of the tree of the knowledge of good and evil." *They no longer require a symbolic interpretation of each moment.* Because of this, it sometimes appears to those observing through the old historical filters that those functioning in the new paradigm are ignoring common sense. But this is never the case.

The behavior of those who function in a state of grace makes perfect sense, but it is sense that is drawn from a higher frequency of awareness. Its logic is not beyond the ego's grasp, but it is of a more rapid vibration than the slower-frequency logic of the ego. For the ego to understand the lightning process through which the spirit reaches a sequence of decisions, it has to break down the process and study it one frame, one step at a time. While this can be done, it is much better to experience instinctual awareness than to analyze it.

The inner guidance of the *life force* embodies a deeper and more ancient sense, a sense common to conscious beings throughout the stars. It comes from a truly Holy Spirit and is the shared property of all those who inhabit the conscious realms. It can be comprehended by those in the old paradigm, but as long as they stay within the old paradigm, they will never know its source within themselves.

The Etheric Antenna

The *word* that God sends into this turning age is metaconceptual, telepathic, both more comprehensive and more specific than linguistic terms. This is the living word of which you have scriptural mention, the luminous living information that inspires those who receive it and nurtures those who welcome it into their lives. In a literal as well as a spiritual sense it is the staple foodstuff, the nourishment of the coming age. It flows outward from your heart to nourish you and all included in your love. It is the understanding of life itself, providing you from within, a quality of individuality that will complement the world around you.

The living information is inseparable from your life force. Biologically, you have experienced the animation of your life force, but you are not truly incarnate until you allow this current into your conscious awareness. Biologically, this energy is the center of your life. As you also allow it to become the center of your consciousness, your emotional realm is activated as an instrument of perception.

Just as the eye is designed to sense and interpret certain frequencies as light, and the ear is designed to sense and interpret other frequencies as sound, the human emotional realm is designed to sense and creatively interpret the motivational, life-bringing energies that radiate throughout the universe.

When you move beyond the vision prisons of historical definitions and release your heart to love, a superbly crafted *etheric antenna* unfolds from the luminous envelope that surrounds your body in light. This antenna behaves like a sensitive plant. When the heart is anxious, when emotions are troubled or turbulent, it remains closed. But when the heart relaxes in love, its delicate gossamer flowers unfold, like a tree coming into bloom, providing you with a sophisticated etheric organ designed to receive the information that circulates in the universal sea of Being.

The seven flowerlike disks of the etheric antenna are anchored in the glands of the endocrine system. These glands bridge spirit and matter. They are the biological receptors that translate the higher-frequency information picked up by the etheric disks (the chakras of yogic tradition) into language the nervous system can recognize. They are designed to audit ultrafine frequencies, bringing both sensory and what some would call extrasensory impressions into your awareness.

The etheric antenna is damaged by violent emotions such as anger or hatred. It is never in any danger from outside emotions, only from your own. It can remain open for months even in the midst of violent emotion, as long as you remain calm and continue to feel love for those around you. However, when your love is withheld, your etheric antenna closes, and then there are no shortcuts. Your heart must be returned again to God; it must resume the expression of love. And even then, time is required before your etheric antenna's full sensitivity is restored.

The fully activated human sensory system is synonymous with your spirit's presence and occupies the same space. It extends beyond those portions of it whose vibratory rate is slow enough to attract the molecular structure of your nervous system. Its spatial reach extends outward from the physical body to include a larger vibratory field, of which the etheric antenna is but a part.

From the spinal trunk the branches of the nervous system reach throughout your body, nurturing the many tiny leaves that are its cells. Its uppermost branches flower into the threefold petals of your human brain. When your love extends to include enough of your world to admit the vision of eternity, you will feel its blossomlike sensors unfolding, blooming to bring you more complete awareness of the multidimensional reality in which you live.

Yet the fully activated human sensory system is more than just an interdimensional communication device. In min-

iature it replicates in the structural pattern of its biogravitational field the same pattern found in planetary, solar, galactic, and universal fields. Activated, as it is for all those in
an awakened state, it is capable of bringing through its own
miniaturized circuitry the awareness of the archangelic beings who overlight each of these spheres. Through it incarnate ones are able to access an experience base and system
of informational exchange common to all universally conscious beings, drawing upon a shared pool of wisdom—and
knowing it as their own. For behind their subjective roles
and specialties, all conscious entities share a common field of
being. They experience the various individual foci in the sea
of that being not as *others* but as features of their own universal wholeness.

Just as the latticework of galactic love, which holds this
cluster of stars suspended, is mirrored above in the vibrational circuitry of this solar system, and then mirrored once
again in the awakening circuitry of planetary intelligence, on
a smaller scale this same basic design pattern—of eternal
love—is mirrored in human biology, thus providing us with
universally compatible systems for the habitation, enjoyment, and continuing creation of these phenomenal realms.

11

The Sensuous Universe

When you remember the play that lifted your heart as a child, you will know the heart of God. You will understand the motives behind this universal expression. God's creations and the interwoven fabric of space and time, which holds them suspended in vibratory dance, may be fraught with what appears to present-day human consciousness as dazzling complexity, but any kitten understands God's motives.

Why do dolphins leap joyful from the sea? Why do the morning birds sing? Why does the earth dance in trees and reach forests to the sun? Why do children play?

The purpose of these realms is enjoyment. This is a recreational universe, designed to multiply the life forms that share God's great passion: *beauty*—its creation and appreciation, its playful development in structure, in symphonies of light, sound, time, and dimension.

Beyond the shadowlands where God and self are seen as heavy and somber, the winds of change bring fresh currents of thought to those whose hearts are whole. Feel the creative melodies of eternity surrounding you, penetrating your envelope of light. As they echo in your soul, know that you are one with the Maker of the music.

Those who live intuitively are guided through the dimensional worlds by a rhythmic undercurrent of inspiration. Inner music guides their outer function, highlighting choices that indicate their most creative patterns of environmental interaction. Through that music flows the joyful current of creation.

The music of creation releases energy, gives energy, gives life itself to all who appreciate it. Biology is not a somber dance. *The universe is deployed in song!* Listen to the melodies crackling through the air around you. Some find their way into human media and drift to you from a radio, an open window, a passing car. Others appear only once in the ethers for your ears alone.

Songs will be your maps in the new world, songs whose rhythms guide the energies of stars. They enter human time tangibly and intangibly, both audibly and telepathically. Their melodies overturn, undermine, and dissolve the structures of historical illusion. Sense their waves, the currents of their energy. Can you discern among them the musical stream of creation that called you into being, the song of individuation sung by eternity at your birth into time, the song that drew you from the fields of singularity?

Drink deeply of the love that comes to you on the currents of this, your definition song. Receive its nourishment, its direction.

As you relax into the expression of love, the center of your self-understanding shifts from your individuality to your universality, from past to present, from ego to spirit. As this shift from self-centeredness to God-centeredness occurs, the thoughts, visions, dreams, and motivational currents of Universal Being come to have greater emphasis than your personality. The polarity of your emotional field shifts from fear to love. Your spirit regains access to your thought processes. Your ego is relieved of its excessive burden of culturally assumed responsibility and is happy and fulfilled, perhaps for the first time in your incarnate experience.

As you learn to draw identity from the life force, your expression becomes the channel through which a steady stream of consciousness flows from Creator into Creation. You become one of God's dimensional terminals, individualizing perfectly for the time and place where you are. Whatever the next developmental step may be, your identity takes the form most able to draw it forth. Your behavior flows out of your instinctual nature. You pick up the tools of your trade and interact with your environment, drawing forth its potential through emotional, mental, and physical movement directed by the music of your soul. This music is never tedious or repetitive but always flowing through chord changes and melodic variations that keep it fresh and alive. The music itself carries the signal to curtail or modify activities long before you grow tired or desirous of a change.

Though the individual music varies, the source of the inner directional music is the same for all those whose lives are motivated by love. When you are working with others who have learned to live in this way, their activities unfold in a relation that is naturally harmonic to your own. While your melodies differ, your rhythms are always aligned. You are able to coordinate your efforts without cumbersome surface-level organization. To the culturally conditioned ego this appears as nothing less than magic, but the principles at work are natural law.

Individual scores blend in the evocation of collective beauty, in the creation of harmonious social forms and new structures of matter, sound, light, and energy. They flow together in the composition of a symphonic society where workplace and recreational environment are one. Those who live in this way do not look upon their occupations as chores or burdens. They make their living through their play.

This is what it means to live in a state of grace.

You currently have no large-scale models or precedents to help you anticipate this on a global scale, but as the peoples of your world return to living in harmony with natural design, they will know neither disease nor want. Even now, before planetary human society as a whole relaxes into this symphonic pattern of being, you can learn to support yourself by doing *what you most love to do*. There is no better way than this to help in easing the transition for the human family.

So long as you remain in identity patterns centered around physicality alone, you remain subliminally afraid of the earth, you have difficulty securing your material needs. You do not know the ease with which the produce of this planetary garden flows to those who love this world. The moment you awaken to the truth of yourself, the moment you realize that you are essentially a spiritual being, your relationship to matter changes. You have no further difficulty drawing to you all that you require.

Those who serve the purposes of life are not troubled for its necessities.

The finest food that this planet has to offer is only a small portion of the nourishment that comes to those who live their lives in the energy currents of eternal love.

The earth recognizes people in whom God flowers. There is a sensuousness, a centeredness, a grace to their movement. There is a relaxed gentility of power flowing quietly within and beneath their action. There is a humble assuredness about them, a reverence, a sense of humor and a sense of the sacred entwined. They are the magical people for whom the earth has longed.

12

The World Economic Sculpture

When you see the chiseled canyon face on Mars, or our reminders in the Andes and the Yucatan, when you fly above the serpent mounds or gaze upon the pyramids, know that in reality none of these symbols, not even the great Mayan calendar, nor the richly symbolic story of our breakthrough teachings on the hills of Galilee, are as significant as *the sculpture of your present world order.*

Art has always imitated (and the finest art has always led to) reality. If you could retreat to some higher ground to gain perspective on human affairs, you would see in your global economy a living sculpture of planetary significance. Like no art before, it is even now leading you and your race from beneath the illusions of a fading order to a new understanding of yourselves and the world.

The present configuration of your world's economic interests has not occurred by chance. Their specific placement has meaning and design. It is a puzzle of sorts, a circuit to short an illusion whose passing is near.

Historical peoples assume their behavior is ordered and rational, yet often we have shepherded entire cultures in specific directions for centuries before even one of their number looked up to note what that direction might be. If people were more perceptive they would recognize the guidance that has brought them and their nations into their present positions on earth. They would know that despite belief systems and ideologies, despite differences in orientation and nationality, each vested interest that will ultimately survive the twentieth century has something of value at its core. It is this essence that we nurture and strengthen until it blossoms like ripened corn and the husk of unreality is stripped away.

In the dawning light of this new millennium, the framework surrounding human affairs can be seen as a chessboard of sorts, each global interest represented by a piece on the board. Each piece, each player, as this new era dawns, is possessed with access to unlimited information. And each knows that using that information intelligently is the key to success. Institutionally invested human interests have at their disposal not merely computer technology to help them organize their information more accurately but also a rising flood of information itself, unprecedented in the history of nations.

A child today with a Christmas computer has more information at her disposal than the Vatican library had at the height of the Renaissance. That same child, for the cost of a phone call, can tap data retention systems and in seconds retrieve information that would have been beyond the reach of the U.S. Defense Department as recently as the close of World War II.

Yet new information technology merely reflects the field of intelligence that is growing upon the earth. It does not cause it. The leaves and branches of the vine reflect an inner genetic design, yet they are neither its architect nor its cause.

There is no breakthrough in information processing that does not have its corresponding realization in human consciousness. And always, the realization appears first. What is tangible appears only after its potential has been observed in human awareness and described in some communicable form. It is possible, therefore, to anticipate coming changes in any human field by monitoring the insights that are finding their way into expression at the creative edge of human thought.

Because of the revolutionary leaps in understanding that have occurred in recent decades in the fields of international diplomacy, ecology, relationship training, sociology, and economics, to name just a few, the fact of humans' interdependence with one another and with the earth has now become widely acknowledged. As the implications of this new awareness of interdependence continue to manifest politically, the inevitable result is only a matter of time. *The fear-centered dynasties that have dominated historical peoples are facing an increasingly well-defined choice: fundamental reevaluation and healthy change—or imminent collapse.*

In nations that recognize this, nations whose leaders have already drawn this conclusion from the direction and momentum of their histories, another conclusion also begins to suggest itself. Unthinkable at first, it is rejected. But it keeps bubbling up again and again. And each time it reappears, the cultural objections are fewer and less convincing than before. What a few great leaders like Gandhi and Martin Luther King saw decades ago is now being realized by many world leaders: *This whole process, this process of fear-centered social orders moving inexorably toward extinction, is intentional. It is not happenstance.*

History has been designed with this particular conclusion in mind.

A New Field of Consciousness

The earth is rapidly entering a new field of consciousness that is bringing it back into resonance with primal rhythms of creation. This new consciousness is rooted not in the historical human understanding of God but in an intelligence that resides within the very animating current of the universe. It is rooted in the informational reality of a universal Presence whose awareness and memory is awakening inside human time, awakening and gazing forth from within each vested interest, each player in this planetary field, helping people to understand the greater context in which they move: the board, the other players, the rules of the Primate into Universal Species game.

When the days begin to lengthen after the winter solstice, you know that summer will surely come. But the change is not immediate. It takes all of winter and spring for the earth to respond. Time is required for land masses to release the chill of winter, for water, soil, and rock to absorb and retain the heat of the sun. And so the inertia of history's chill requires a season to dissolve, though the cause of that dissolution is already present and active.

Cresting as a wave between the years 1987 and 1989, a new and greater love washes over the earth. Riding upon that wave an influx of new consciousness enters your planetary field, bringing perspective and understanding to those who are attuned through their love. Yet it will be nearly two decades before the full effects of this new influx of consciousness are felt, before its implications are fully embodied, before the new understanding is transformed from precept to reality.

For millennia, successive waves of spirit beings have come to this planet to assist humankind's processes of historical education. But the influx of consciousness that rides upon this current wave is more powerful than any that came before.

This is the beginning of the time of our descent and the age of your awakening, the time when spirit and ego harmoniously integrate, the time spoken of in ancient cultures as the era of the gods' return. The peoples of the earth have glimpsed its coming and viewed it through the distorting filters of their indigenous terms and labels, yet the event itself is larger than any human system of understanding, broader than any cultural description.

We are aligning our fields of perception with all those who are able to understand themselves in real terms: those who have learned to identify not with the body, but with the spirit who animates the body. In the end the question of whether it is they who awaken or we who incarnate loses all relevance, for the spell is broken, the shell of historical illusion is shattered, and a new creature emerges, blinking in the light of a truly new day.

Trust in the wisdom that designed the intricacies of the human body and the exquisite ordering of the galaxies, and these next years will unfold their petals before you like a flower opening to the sun rays of that new and brighter day. Trust in God once again and your understanding will be as the fragrance of that flower. You will have no need to fear. Do not be concerned if you falter, if you make mistakes. Pay no heed to those who call to you from behind. Move wholeheartedly beyond historically manufactured thought into the thought currents of the Universal Intelligence that is awakening in this planetary sphere.

Remain in your walk, your station, especially if it touches the government of a nation. Do not leave your work. Stay. Bring light into your world. Do your work with greater consciousness and you will naturally rise in your profession, even as the sun of a dawning consciousness rises in the people around you. Do not wait for yourself or the world to change. Accept today. Harvest the fullness of its promise. This is all you can do, yet it is all that needs to be done.

Help us to minimize the disruption of terrestrial systems of production and distribution, while working to transform them incrementally, as we have been transforming other and older structures these centuries past. The old orders are turning away from fear—for their own interests they are turning—away from manipulation and exploitation. They are discovering satisfying new structures in service, education, healing. In the greater effectiveness of these new structures they are finding the prosperity and success that eluded them when their motives were not in the interests of all.

You who are designed to work within the present systems of human power are the eyes that look forth from the towers of the knights and pawns, castles and bishops on the chessboard. You are the lights of those worlds. Do not abandon your posts or it may seem to the subjects of those powers that they too are abandoned. Too rapid a breakdown of production or distribution would deprive them of the time they need to perceive their state for what it is. Those who have been programmed to accept a feudal order may need your presence—and a little time—to awaken. You are the keepers of the old orders' gates. Make entry difficult. Allow all to leave who will. Outside the earth is fertile, the season full.

Others of you choose not to work within those structures. All about the chessboard of interacting global interests you are building a new and benign environment. Landscapers, caretakers in the universal garden of magnificence, moving more freely than kings and queens, more mobile than knights of old, you note that the chessboard and its historical players intrude upon but one small corner of the grounds. You are like flowers and herbs, like trees growing beneath and around the edges of the board, even as others are like grasses springing up within. The board itself grows annually more illumined, spiraling upward, outward as the millennium dawns, beyond its two-dimensional symbolism, its sixty-four squares flowing into the sixty-four hexagrams of the *I Ching*, the sixty-four nucleotides of the genetic code, spiraling, swirling, each luminous square animated, multidimensional, alive.

The context in which historical institutions exist has already experienced a fundamental change. Human assumptions are themselves shifting. Before this quarter-century transition has passed, humans will understand in wholly different terms both themselves and the world in which they live. The very ground of being will be perceived through the transformed vision of wholeness. Human consciousness itself will be illumined in the Presence of the One who is awakening in this planetary field.

This awakening at the end of history is of such power and of such awesome magnitude that its approach has been noticeably altering human affairs for nearly twenty centuries. As a causal force, its shock waves ripple backward through time, drawing all historical events toward it as a magnetic field draws filings of iron.

This event, anticipated by Christians as the Second Coming of Christ, is in fact the *first fully conscious incarnation* of the Eternal One in the collective consciousness of a world's biosphere. Jesus came to help prepare human understanding for this event, to herald it as the morning star heralds the dawn. But the dawn whose light is growing on the future horizon requires all of humankind, indeed, all of biology, to shine full—and such a dawn has no precedent.

As this event approaches ever nearer, all human organizations rooted in fear will be faced with increasing structural difficulties until they either change, restructure, or collapse.

Those who subscribe to illusions of supremacy, whether racial, religious, national, or otherwise, will share in the destabilization and disarray of their economies and their organizations as all systems rooted in such illusion continue to dissolve. With their belief in systems external to themselves, trusting in human concepts and institutions instead of in the living God within them, such individuals will be found wanting as their systems collapse.

Yet there are few human organizations that do not have at their core a genuine vision of value, which, if not initially defined in service or in love, can now be redefined with the greater clarity of those who seek to ease their society's passage into the new. These organizations will experience not the destruction of systems that contain no one of perception but rather the more gentle restructuring that occurs when there is conscious human participation and a desire to preserve and build upon the best of what has been.

Should you find yourself with influence over existing systems of production, resource management, or exchange, know that you have not come to such a position by accident. On the deepest level of your eternal spirit, a level of identity you may or may not yet be aware of, you have chosen this. Long ago, you chose to be among those of us who would steward the resources of this world during these potentially turbulent times of transition. It is by choice that you are now in a position to facilitate the equitable distribution of essential goods and services, thereby helping to lessen adjustment difficulties during these years of fundamental reorientation.

During the two remaining decades of this transition—the 1990s and the 2000s—many of your current systems for producing and distributing the necessities of life will remain important. Even into the millennium after awakening, some of them will continue to be of value. Yet the harmony that will come to the nations of the earth by the end of this cycle will not be the superficial harmony of a well-managed empire. It will be a harmony at once deeper and more sublime, radiating from within all things, a spiritual harmony pervading spheres both manifest and unmanifest, a symphonic current of cooperative exchange, benefiting all.

The approach of spirit causes an intensification, a quickening of vibration on the perceptual frequencies that provide personal as well as collective human awareness. As the vibrational rates of these frequencies intensify, it becomes more difficult to maintain a life or an institution organized arbitrarily along the currents of fear, for such patterns are foreign to the awakened human nature that is emerging. Centers of greed and corruption, long ignored or taken for granted, are exposed. To some, matters may even appear to worsen for a while, but wounds must be cleaned before they can heal.

Before the graceful symmetry of an enlightened economic order can replace the dusty stagnation of a closed society, there must be movement. When the windows are opened in the spring and the breeze enters the house, replacing the stale air of winter with the fresh air of a new season, it naturally stirs up the dust. But it would be a foolish housekeeper who would leave the windows closed all summer for fear of a little dust. The winds of change must flow freely around all structures to sculpt them anew. New challenges will naturally arise along with the new freedom and openness. For a time it may even seem to some as if security and stability have gone to the wind. Yet this cannot be prevented. The consciousness that is arriving here to awaken in human affairs is that of a *moving* Being. Yours is not a stationary God.

So it is that the winds of change blow more strongly through human affairs during the Great 1987–1989 Revelations. You have anticipated this as the time when the changes experienced on personal levels during the 1960s and 1970s transmissions would begin to appear in government, international banking, and multinational corporate affairs. These changes have begun. They will continue throughout the next two decades, gradually making the human world over in the consciousness of love, openness, honesty, equality of rights, and opportunity for all.

During this coming twenty-year cycle, in most parts of the world more progress will be made than many now believe possible in areas such as human rights, ecological awareness, disarmament, education, free elections, and the fulfillment of basic human needs for food and water.

But there will be a few locations that hold out, pockets of resistance. And in these places conditions will worsen up to the moment of collective awakening. It is not negativism to state this: Shadows become more clearly defined as the light grows. The brush of education may help to soften the edge of shadow in some of these instances. International sanctions will help in others. However, most people will find their greatest leverage for positively affecting their world in those nations where the political structure encourages the currents of new awareness.

There are a few—they know who they are—who are called on to directly address the Beiruts and Belfasts of the world. Take care. Too much distraction with pockets of negativity can dissipate your energy, blind you to the larger global perspective, and greatly reduce the service that you might otherwise offer.

When there lie before you dozens of opportunities to apply your energies, skills, talents, and insights, opportunities that assure you of having a positive impact on people's lives, as well as on the earth and her creatures, it is not generally wise to invest your time in situations where you do not have the invitation or cooperation of those whom you seek to benefit.

Observe which nations are allowing new leadership and new awareness to guide them. Notice how certain communities, cities, even whole societies are stepping beyond the fearful paradigms of the past. This is not insignificant. The new consciousness is arising phoenixlike in the midst of the old. Your world is being healed. It is becoming whole.

No system of government in the historical condition has been perfect, but many systems, often ideologically quite different, contain within them the seeds of perfection.

Those who look with a deeper vision see familiar figures moving beneath the platforms and behind the stage props. Listening for the truth amidst the surface clamor, they hear the angelic inspirations behind socialism and know they are the same voices that inspire democracy, the same voices that have always encouraged people to break the yokes of tyranny, politically and in the more subtle government of the soul. Your world has moved through much during this most recent cycle of education, but do not forget: Even during historical times the greatest movements have been not political, but spiritual.

13

A New Order of the Ages

We are not in much direct contact yet with government officials, nor with world bankers and international financiers. Our first contacts with them will occur during the more powerful transmissions of 1987 to 1989.

—THE STARSEED TRANSMISSIONS, DECEMBER 31, 1978

*T*he replication of another generation in the image of the former is no longer possible. The current generation of young will drink but shallow draughts at the fount of illusion, if they drink at all. For the perceptive of your race have felt the changing climate of the world. And they have realized that in this new climate generational duplication would not perpetuate their societies but terminate them.

It is in the interest of every government, democratic or otherwise, to cooperate with the changes of these times and to allow their young people to pursue options and develop capacities beyond those available in societies in which ideas and identities are mass produced.

The stability of a government is not threatened but increased by those of its citizens who become conscious.

Ruling interests will not necessarily be dissolved during these decades of transition. However, if they wish to remain solvent through these times and on into the posthistoric era, they must recognize and adjust to the intensifying frequencies of love. For institutional solvency now hinges upon the ability to restructure along the vibrational lines of the intensifying energy field of awakening consciousness, in patterns compatible with the many diverse forms that love can take. Not only will this assure their survival, but, more important, it will assist the overall human transition from the fear-dominated historical order to the new order of love-centered creation. Their skill at this and the degree of consciousness with which they participate will determine the level of their prosperity.

Though present-day systems of government must evolve further before they fully represent and embody the spirits of their respective peoples, they are nevertheless a vast improvement upon the tyranny—and in many cases, the absolute tyranny—that preceded them.

How easily some forget. How near to you even now are men and women who remember living under the emperors, the tsars, the fear dynasties of the early decades of this century. You can be sure that those who remember the times before the old orders were shaken do not wish for their return.

The actual and legal protection of basic human rights is still being established in many nations of the world. But a century ago in those same nations such rights were not even conceived of, certainly not among those who governed. What the founders of your present systems have wrought has been imperfect, to be sure, but the movements they have initiated are far from complete and their direction is healthy.

Wherever our influence extends, the process of democratization continues; the recognition of human equality grows, along with a passion for liberty and a sense of personal involvement in the collective human destiny. Those whom we touch no longer feel that they are passive observers of human events. They realize the transformative power of truth, when it is honored, lived, and articulated sincerely. They become involved.

The next two decades will see the many sprouts of democracy that have struggled through the spring thaws of these past two centuries come into summer flower. These will not be decades without challenge, immune to economic uncertainty or political upheaval, but so it must be. For these are decades of promise and transformation, decades slowly filling—even now it has begun—with the consciousness of the Presence of God.

In this growing field of consciousness, harmony is empowered and given authority to stabilize cultural, political, and social revolutions that a short time ago could not have occurred without violence. Along with deeper terrestrial processes and the currents that rule human affairs, world events are gradually being drawn into resonance with the steadily growing field of planetary awareness—even before the critical moment *when that field itself jells in the cohesive realization of its singularity.*

The histories of your present nation-states, though they are fraught with intrigue and distorted by the fears of troubled human egos, are histories nevertheless—for those who choose to examine them through the eyes of the spirit—of vastly improving conditions for the peoples of your world. On every continent, the workers of the 1990s are far better off than they were in the 1930s or the 1950s, to say nothing of conditions a century ago. Spiritually, economically, politically, they enjoy conditions today that yesterday existed only in the minds of their visionaries.

Your present world is built on assumptions inconceivable to your ancestors.

Yet it is good that you do not rest on yesterday's progress, that you seek to move on, to better conditions for yourselves and your children. We support you in this deepening. We encourage you and provide you with the insights required to further build your dreams, for in truth the assumptions upon which the present human world rests need to continue on in the currents of change. But do not deny the gains earned by those who came before you.

Your governments, for all their failings, are reflections of the hopes and fears of the people they govern.

As your hopes become shared visions and evolve into realizable strategies, your fears will continue to diminish. Your governments will continue their metamorphoses into ever deeper actualizations of democracy and the principles of equality in which it is rooted.

The health of a nation's governing structure is directly related to how much it is guided by the great lesson of history: *For every violent change, there is an equal and opposite pain, a price paid by victors and vanquished alike.*

Military Power

Until the moment of final awakening when the field of planetary consciousness jells in cohesive realization, military power will continue to be a necessity for all but a few nations.

The purpose of military power is to minimize violence: to ensure that the strong do not prey upon the weak; to use its force, when necessary, to ensure that small ruling elites do not exploit communities; to halt explosions of ethnic violence while simultaneously using statecraft and diplomacy to address and rectify the imbalances that always underlie such explosions. These are valid and, for a short time yet, still essential uses of military power.

A military occupation that enforces an imbalanced and inequitable status quo is counterproductive, whereas an occupation that disarms opposing factions while facilitating between them negotiations that address the underlying currents of contention is truly a peace-keeping and, if it does its job well, a *temporary* force.

Whenever a military presence extends overlong there has been a failure to bring contending parties into meaningful negotiation or to allow them sufficient freedom of expression.

Governments weak in negotiative intelligence who attempt to compensate militarily for their weakness have been declining since the 1960s. Pacific nations, meanwhile, have been prospering and will continue to prosper as this transition progresses.

In an age of information when new consciousness illumines the ancient corridors of power, and even the darkest places embrace openness and change, the leaders of most nations are realizing that, except in self-defense, violence always proves counterproductive. It is becoming obvious that communication, not confrontation, is the wave of the future and, indeed, the new human frontier.

Warfare is a form of communication, a primitive signaling strategy used to resolve disagreements—usually between peoples who speak different languages or think in incompatible ideological modes. It is expensive and notoriously inefficient.

When far less expensive computer-based communication technology can cut through language barriers, instantly identifying the imbalances underlying any dispute and offering multiple scenarios of resolution, there is no longer a need for war, especially given the unacceptable costs of a nuclear conflict.

Advanced communication technology can project with frightening accuracy exactly what a given war would achieve, the probable outcome, the cost to society, and approximately how many decades a recovery would require. It can itemize the resources, human and other, that would be irrevocably lost in a projected conflict. When such projections can be made cheaply and accurately, economics alone are enough to retire war as a tool of communication. This may be news to many, but among high-level military personnel this information has been circulating for some time. As a result, the intelligence level of world leaders has been noticeably upgraded in recent years, as has the entire level of

113

international exchange. While popular culture continues to see armed conflict as a viable way of settling differences, warfare is rapidly becoming obsolete, an artifact of preinformational times.

The Decline of Tyranny and Repression

In most cases those who govern the democratic republics of the world sincerely desire to create a better human community. We do what we can to strengthen and assist the clarification of such motives. Wherever power elites dissolve before the pressures of these changing times, wherever aristocracies or dictatorships are in the process of becoming open market democracies, wherever entrenched financial interests are losing their ability to control and manipulate disproportionate shares of terrestrial resources, you see people who are being influenced to one degree or another by our energies of awakening. Their activities, though still perhaps tainted with some subconsciousness, are at their cores motivated by the growing awareness of the One whom most of them cannot yet call God.

At the beginning of Western civilization, the materializing forces had structured the patterns of fear to restrain, to hold back, to harness as much as possible the approaching field of eternal consciousness. The early breakthroughs of clear thought in the warrior nations of the West were harnessed by the Roman Empire and later by the monolithic feudalism of the "Christian" monarchs. Our teachings could not remove that restraint, but they could and did modify it. They weakened its hold. Even as the feudal "lords of the earth" attempted to use truth to further their own ends, truth used them and spread despite their attempts to regulate and control it.

The first breakthroughs of objective thought were imperfectly translated, practiced, and understood, but enough of their influence seeped through to cause these past two millennia to become times of declining influence for fear-ruling elites.

Tyrants still appeared, but the duration of their tyrannies came to be measured in months instead of decades, in years instead of hereditary dynasties. And wherever there were those who attempted to manipulate and control the energies of human exchange, their way grew more difficult.

Self-righteousness defeats the purpose it presumes to serve. Those who fight what they despise with deception only strengthen its hold, sowing the seeds of further deception, which then have no course but to grow and appear in yet another decade or generation, presenting yet another opportunity to be seen clearly and resolved. Resolution on the first occasion requires more deliberation in the short term, for it forces the deeper issues up into the awareness of those who may prefer not to see them. Yet it is the only path to long-term resolution.

Approaches that merely mask the symptoms of inequality are far more destructive than the perpetrators of those approaches generally realize, for beneath their veneers inequality continues to exist, and there, hidden in the darkness, it grows until it surfaces to explode again in yet another and stronger upheaval.

Did Sherman's march to the sea bring the ravages and hardships of the U.S. Civil War to a more rapid conclusion? Or did it create such deep-seated prejudice and animosity that another century was required for the nation's healing?

The end justifies the means only in the logic of deceit. Wherever evil is chosen in any form, it sows everywhere about it the seeds of its opposing evil. In the end it does not deliver; it consumes.

The choice of love may not always seem the swiftest path to the resolution of difference, but it is the only certain one.

The October revolution; the storming of the Bastille: Examples abound of instances in which the powerful creative energies that we were introducing into the patterns of existing national structures became exaggerated by those who were the stewards of those energies. The stewards were thrown off balance by a success for which they were not prepared. Often they accomplished the initial purpose of the transformative energies—removing the tsars from power in Russia, removing the kings from France—and then unwittingly provoked the chaos that follows self-righteousness with the precision of a shadow. In the end they inhibited the arrival of the very social equality that they sought and truly desired to create.

Those of you who wield the powers of transformation during these times must learn from the excesses of those who have wielded lesser powers before you. Use your powers with humility and with compassion, or you will lose them to those who regard *love for enemies* in terms more immediate than your own.

In cases where the influences of education do not prevail, you will be given the power to remove those who maintain patterns of dominance and exploitation. Do not be afraid of this power. Be decisive in your use of it, but use it always in love, and do not stop halfway.

Remove both dictators and the imbalances that allow them to exist. And when you have succeeded, extend to them the same forgiveness that you yourself have already received. Wherever possible enlist them as helpers, advisers, and cocreative agents in the continued restructuring of the nation. Respect will win them over more surely than corrective measures. Give them the opportunity. Their insight into areas where your own experience is limited may prove vital to you in effecting a smooth transition.

Today's intent counts far more than yesterday's failings. In the eyes of God it is all that counts, for in reality it is all there is. Avoid backlash from those whom you have removed from power or from those who once supported them. Welcome all into the light of the dawning order, knowing that an ocean of public support provides far more effective social regulation than any amount of legislation or punishment. If the structures of a nation's government are not built upon a broad social base, they do not endure. Sense the skills and talents, the strengths and weaknesses of each one, then let each participate according to his or her ability. This will greatly expand the talent pool available to support your efforts, and stabilization will occur more rapidly because of it. Where you see repentance, sincerity, and the demonstration of genuine goodwill, value it. Use it as wisely as any other resource.

Just as the progression of the last two thousand years has made it increasingly difficult for aristocracies—rich and powerful ruling families—to exploit masses of people, so, too, on a subtler level it is making it ever more difficult for governments to be too far out of tune with the voice and spirit of the people they politically represent.

Government derives its sole authority—and the legitimacy of its power— from the will and spirit of its people. When a government loses rapport with the people it governs, it must change or be changed. It is too unstable to remain. Repression in such cases is as futile as sealing the lid on a pressure cooker while stoking the fire beneath; no matter how many bolts (or troops) attempt to keep the lid on, the very laws of nature rule against it.

Repression might delay a nation's movement for a short while—and in an age of electronic media that time is far shorter than it once was—but it cannot prevent it. Repression will only multiply the difficulties associated with realignment when the populist movement inevitably breaks free to release its pent-up desire for change.

Yet repression is not always the response of tyrants. Often it is an unconsidered, knee-jerk reaction, not thought through or planned, a reaction that the government involved quickly sees as an error, but which it feels it must nevertheless defend and uphold to preserve credibility and respect.

This sort of logic was dubious even when the pharaohs ruled Egypt. In today's electronically altered media culture it is antiquated and self-defeating. Honesty and openness offer the only certain route to credibility. People tire of those who always insist that they are right, while in the present climate of change they generally support those who admit mistakes, make intelligent adjustments, and move on.

Where repressive regimes have begun to feel the growing and potentially explosive power of the people they presume to represent, and their leaders seek to avoid the pending explosion, the pressure cooker analogy cautions that it is as unwise to suddenly remove the lid as it was to put it there in the first place. Repressive measures should be removed gradually over a period of weeks or months, with honesty and candor from government leaders, explaining to those affected what they are doing and why. They should begin with immediate changes that demonstrate their sincerity, and then commit themselves to a specific timetable of future changes, securing the agreement of all concerned.

Even the worst government provides services that if suddenly abandoned would create hardship. It is important that there be a time of transition. Difficulties are minimized in slower shifts of power. Even then, it may be too late to entirely avoid violence from the extremes, but a once-repressive government can rest assured that the violence associated with its voluntary dissolution will be much less than the violence that would have occurred had its leaders attempted to retain power.

Times of shifting leadership are often volatile. Those associated with the old government share responsibility with those who represent the new to create a smooth transition. To minimize potential violence, it is wise to focus public attention on incoming rather than outgoing leadership.

It is always prudent to invest more attention in the future than in the past.

Justice can proceed with wisdom. Revenge cannot. Revenge has the ability to divert otherwise creative public sentiment into passions that can easily run out of control. Where power has been relinquished voluntarily, forgiveness, rehabilitation, and education will serve national purposes. If legal proceedings are in order in relation to former leaders, they should certainly not occupy more of the national awareness than the opportunities and possibilities presented by the new order. After the French Revolution, such misplaced emphasis sidetracked and nearly discredited a noble vision.

National Psychology

The psychology of a nation can be healthy or unhealthy, much as that of an individual. The study of *national psychology* has emerged in recent years as the newest and, for now, the most important branch of the social sciences. Many of the same criteria that have been used to evaluate the health of individuals are now being applied to nations. The resulting insights—often *revelations*, in every sense of the term—are leading to new, enlightened, and far more productive national and international policies.

Few outside the intelligence agencies of the industrialized nations are accustomed to thinking of countries as collective entities that can "get sick" just as any other life form can, but this sort of thinking has already terminated the cold war. Its increasing application in the years ahead will revolutionize the field of international diplomacy much as Einstein's theory of relativity revolutionized the field of physics. During the 1920s, for example, both Germany and Japan had specific national disorders. If these disorders had been properly diagnosed and realistically addressed by the rest of the international community—and if certain reasonable adjustments had been granted by those who controlled what was then the British Empire—World War II would not have taken place.

The past cannot be changed, but the present and future are being affected profoundly by this growing awareness. A nation's psychological health is vital to the happiness and prosperity of its people. Leaders and opinion shapers, both in and out of government, have a responsibility to promote policies and perspectives that lead to national health. It is no coincidence that such perspectives reflect the truth. The truth promotes health just as surely as deceit produces disease.

The truth is never contained in opposing ideologies. Truth is the reality that overlights all *healthy* opposition.

In the affairs of a nation there is a need for diversity of views and opinions. Healthy views and opinions may diverge 180 degrees on an issue yet still encourage creative exchange and promote equitable national policy. The spokes of a wheel diverge 180 degrees, yet they are precisely what give the wheel its strength. In order for an eagle to fly, its wings must reach out equally in opposite directions. An eagle with a broken wing, like a totalitarian state, is unhealthy.

The new science of national psychology recognizes that in the affairs of a contiguous human community, there are *unhealthy* views and opinions. Their primary feature, as well as their common denominator, is intolerance. Unhealthy views and opinions do not grant the validity, or even the possible validity, of any other view. They emphasize division. They lead to lopsided, destructive, and often ethnocentric policies that favor elites and diminish freedoms.

There can be a broad spectrum of healthy, diverse viewpoints, all contributing to the balanced progress of a nation. And there can be an equally broad spectrum of diseased viewpoints leading only to hatred, violence, and division.

Health—or its absence—does not lie in perspectives themselves but in the hearts of those who hold those perspectives. Where alternate views are respectfully exchanged and considered, the nation prospers. Where those very same views are exchanged in anger or in fear, the nation suffers. When a government ceases to tolerate diversity of views, curtails freedom of expression, and censors its media, the people of that nation have a responsibility to either change their government or establish another. This is more than a right; it is a sacred trust.

The articulation of vision is the first order of business for any new government. If that vision is to succeed in establishing and maintaining rapport with its people, it must include in its very preamble (in nations where such things are not already established) specific and legally irreversible mechanisms to guarantee the freedom of media, the freedom of elections, the preservation of basic human rights, the assurance of universal legal equality to its citizens regardless of race, sex, religion, nationality, or social, economic, or lifestyle distinction, and last, but equally vital, assurance that all of the people under that government's jurisdiction have equal access to the basic requirements of life.

While the communist and the developing nations of the world have more often suffered from governments not sufficiently responsive to their populations, in the United States and in a few other nations, the other extreme has occasionally been experienced. This occurs when a government attempts to please the whims and passing fancies of its people rather than their genuine needs. It is the result of insecure and often inexperienced politicians who lack the courage to act always in accordance with their highest vision; instead they allow their decision making to be determined by what they imagine the people want.

A politician is not a leader.

Those who are more concerned with elections than with what they believe to be in the best interests of the people they represent lack the vision and integrity that would qualify them as true leaders. A leader always acts according to his or her vision, considering carefully the views and feelings of his or her constituency, sensing the overlighting wholeness of those views, how they converge like the spokes of a wheel in the central hub of balance that is the truth. And then the leader acts upon what he or she genuinely believes to be in the best long-term interests of the society, the environment, and all who may be affected.

A leader may appear in the field of politics, as well as in any other field, but a true leader is not controlled by elections or opinion polls.

A true leader is attuned to the deeper long-term rhythms that pulse through the collective heart and is inspired and guided by them. He or she is not overly impressed with superficial fluctuations or with those who all too readily fall under their spell. A good leader knows that as the systems of production and exchange of the earth's nations become increasingly entwined in a single global economy, vision that remains local, or even national, in scope may yet be myopic in terms of planetary realities.

The politico-economic climate of this world has only recently entered the maelstrom of history's final decades. The pace of change will continue to accelerate until the second decade of the 21st century. A good leader will facilitate rather than ignore what is essentially the most fundamental revolution since humankind was distinguished from its mammalian cousins.

In a healthy society, economy always follows ecology, and education precedes them both.

14

A Moment of Quantum Awakening

*A*t the moment of quantum awakening, change will occur rapidly, rippling across the terrestrial surface like a wave. Everything in the earth's gravitational field will be affected in some way. This will be a time of massive change, of change on a scale that has no historical precedent, though it does have antecedents in the prehistoric events of this and of distant worlds. The changes that your generation will experience before it passes the torch to another are more fundamental than those that accompanied the agricultural revolution—and those changes took thousands of years. They are more far-reaching than the changes of industrialization, which took nearly three centuries to transpire. Yet, deep and fundamental, massive though these present changes are, they will occur within the span of just a single human life.

Properly understood, these changes and their coming have the ability to inspire a degree of hope and optimism unprecedented in the history of your race; for they spell the end of humankind's subconscious condition and therefore portend, as the scriptures of the world foretell, an end to bloodshed, starvation, warfare, exploitation, and needless suffering.

Within your lifetime you will witness revelations that will show the foolishness of much that was once deemed wise. You will watch as traditions and historical habit patterns once assumed to be survival imperatives are discovered to be detriments to a healthy life and to a healthy society.

Behavior that made sense for creatures who imagined they were islands of individuality is abandoned by those who experience the interconnectivity of all life. The consciousness that is awakening upon this world is no respecter of Darwinian values. Its perception brings new values and new ways of being. During these decades you are seeing the descent of the Angels of Healing. Even now, all around you—and perhaps in your own life—they are incarnating. In some cases these are beings who have not known human form since before the descent of historical time.

It is possible that you are among those who have held only a tenuous and flickering connection with your incarnational successions. It is no matter for judgment. Those who incarnate now, those who bring the fullness of their eternal talents, attributes, and perspectives into today's people, are the agents of healing. They alone have it in their power to experience this awesome time of transition as glorious or traumatic. All are invited to remember their essence, their purpose, their reason for being here, and to bring through into this age of transformation the sense of celebration that invariably accompanies such remembrance.

Our numbers upon the earth have grown rapidly since our first large-scale arrivals began in the late 1960s. Yet it is not quantity, not numbers that will make the difference, but the quality of our compassion, the quality of the love that radiates from our hearts.

Every individual who becomes a clear and undistorted channel for eternal love into these times offsets a thousand who remain locked in the dissolving values of the old.

We are rapidly dispelling what remains of human illusion, helping all to identify with the growing currents, the energies, and the forces of love and life. You are already living in the dawning hours of the Age of Planetary Awakening, the age of peace and community building. It is here now for those sensitive to its fragrance, texture, majesty, and vision.

The age has begun when the earth is to be cultivated like a flower garden and her gifts presented as conscious offerings to the gardeners of eternal beauty, the age when humankind returns its gifts to the earth, to her soil, her streams, her mountains, her oceans, her creatures of water, air, fire, and clay.

The future, as always, holds an element of surprise. Yet some things are as certain as the movement of the stars.

A mother never knows exactly what hour she will give birth to her child, but she has a "due date," an approximate time when the baby is expected and will most likely be born. For millennia now there have been those in various traditions of both East and West who have known that the earth has a due date sometime during the second decade of the twenty-first century. Though there will be much awakening of individuals prior to the first unified movement of the awakened planetary organism, this movement, like a first breath, will occur in but a single moment. It is then that the Star Maker will consciously awaken in all systems of human biocircuitry capable of sustaining universal awareness.

Babies are sometimes born early, sometimes late. So be aware, be vigilant. Do not discount the possibility that the moment might come as a thief in the night. And do not be among the foolish who will wait until the last moment to come to terms with the rising awareness. This is to be an important occasion.

It is the event that is central to all of human history.

Our emphasis for many thousands of years now has been and continues to be to prepare you for this single moment. For though the changes will be dramatic, they need not be traumatic. Though they will bring a fundamental human revisioning of reality's nature, this need not be perceived as threatening. Essentially, it is a positive and joyous event. The consciousness that will ultimately emerge will be the consciousness of the Eternal One, the Creator, the Being of Life, awake and aware for the first time inside a material universe. Human circuitry is designed to accommodate this consciousness. In much the same way that your individual cells understand their relationship to you, each awakened human being understands him- or herself in hologramatic relationship to this unified field of awareness.

Since this perception of self differs significantly from historical perception, its emergence in collective human consciousness presents the potential for disorientation in those who might react to its coming in fear. We have much to do before the preparation of human consciousness is complete. Still, even if the awakening were to occur in this very moment with no further preparation, it would be an event of unprecedented beauty. However, in that case fewer people would be in a position to appreciate it. We wish to maximize enjoyment and minimize discomfort for all concerned. If human beings understand more fully what is occurring, they will be less likely to react in ways that would cause them unnecessary discomfort.

Regardless of whether one accepts this change or attempts to back away from it, *this event will be of greater power than any the earth has ever seen.* More energy will be released in a very few moments than is typically released upon the surface of the earth in many years. This energy will take the form of heightened perception and deepened emotional connection, rejoining the individual and God.

Though this unprecedented time of intensified energy radiation still lies a few years before you, you are already near enough to it and the event itself is so powerful that time is behaving with increasing subjectivity, bubbling and warping, creating *islands of the future* wherever there are those who deliberately invoke the energies of the emerging consciousness and demonstrate willingness to live their lives in love. These are not disconnected islands beneath the receding seas of historical illusion. They are united in a veritable continent of rising awareness.

As the new reality comes fully into human consciousness (at that moment when the Creator's luminous field comes into perfect alignment with the Earth Mother), all illusion of a destructive nature will be dissolved. Though there have been many centuries leading up to this moment, when the moment comes it will be decisive.

There will be a great shift then, a single moment of quantum awakening. In this moment, the smallest interval of time measured in these dimensions—the interval that occurs in every atom between each of its billions of oscillations per second—will be lengthened unto infinity. An interval of *nontime* will expand. Through that expansion eternity will flow. Some will experience this moment as minutes or hours, others as a lifetime. Still others will experience this flash of nontime as a succession of many lives, and some few will, in this moment, know the Nagual itself, the great nameless Presence that exists before and after all these worlds.

In the expanse of the nontime interval, human beings will have all the time they require to realize, experience, and remember the full consciousness of their eternal spirits and to recall the origin of their individuality in the primordial fields of being. All will have ample time to recharge their form identity and its biological projection with the awareness of who they are, why they have individualized, and why they have chosen to associate with this planet's human expression. Each one will have the choice to return to biological form or to remain in the fields of disincarnate awareness.

Those who choose to return to human form will do so fully aware of who they are. No longer will they be but partially incarnate; they will resume biological residence with the full memory and consciousness of their eternal natures, sharing the creative capacities of the Star Maker, whose reflective cells they will then know themselves to be.

Subconscious orientation in fear will be replaced by conscious orientation in love. The sudden release of power, as the polarity of the collective human emotional field shifts from outer to inner orientation, cannot be avoided no matter how smoothly we seek to guide this transition. All will feel an unmistakable surge of power in the instant of quantum awakening. This is as inevitable as the daily rotation of the earth's continents into and out of the light of the sun.

But the effects? The implications? There is no way to predict them. They depend on the choices you make today.

By extrapolating current trends of consciousness we can establish a probable range of effects. But there may be as many as eight billion people incarnate at that moment, each with complete freedom of choice. And though the choices each one makes in his or her lifetime prior to that moment will certainly predispose that person in one direction or another, there are no guarantees, no assurances.

The spiritual polarity of collective human consciousness did shift once before, triggering a reversal of the earth's magnetic field, a shifting in the position of the poles, and a great deal of destruction. However, that shift was a shift from consciousness to subconsciousness.

We will have a degree of control during this conscious shift that was absent then and so do not expect the same sort of cataclysmic shock waves. Still, it would be underestimating the variables to assume that earth changes will not accompany this event. Almost certainly some will. These will be for the most part of a benevolent nature—a melting of the polar ice caps, for example, bringing rain to arid regions and helping to cleanse toxins from polluted lakes and rivers, a warming and simultaneous moistening of climate that will open to agriculture the extensive plains and fertile river valleys of Greenland, Antarctica, and certain of the world's deserts.

To minimize the trauma of this moment both for you and for others of the human family, it is important that you prepare for it well ahead of time, establishing the habits that will leave your self-understanding fluid, relaxed, and trusting in the overall benevolence of the universe and its resident intelligence.

The best way to prepare for any future moment in time is to be fully in your present moment now.

The only habit you must cultivate, though it may go against the programming and traditions of your society, is to allow into your consciousness the relaxed flow of attention that brings you a clear and accurate picture of the phenomenal world and continuous awareness of the Eternal Presence from which it has unfolded. Such a state of consciousness will allow you to enjoy the rushing energy currents and heightened awareness that will sweep through the earth during the expansion of the nontime interval and will maximize the stabilizing influence that radiates from you into your local surroundings.

Long before the moment of collective awakening there will have been established a sufficient core of people functioning on higher frequencies of awareness to enable the harmonic currents of their respective amplified radiations to displace the influence of those who may react in fear, both at the moment of collective awakening and beforehand. The frequency radiations or vibratory emissions of fear are not harmonious. Their effect on collective human consciousness increases at an arithmetical rate (1, 2, 3, 4, etc.) for each additional person whose behavior is centered in fear, but they do not build in the kind of geometric progression (2, 4, 8, 16, etc.) that is characteristic of the harmonic radiations of love.

Before the final instant of planetary awakening, the radiations of love will constitute the predominant vibrational influence on collective human consciousness, even while a numerical majority remains centered in historical orientation. That condition is now very near.

You who are motivated by love bring to bear on collective human awareness an influence much greater than your historical reason might suppose. Individually you have an impact on the collective predispositions of your species far greater than that of those who are merely trodding the time-worn paths of self-centeredness. You who do your best to make your decisions out of love, who refuse to be controlled by the subconscious machinations of fear, who take time, if necessary, in difficult situations to proceed slowly, consciously, lovingly, are truly among our own. Your awareness of these things will soon be full. You are one upon whom we can depend during the coming shift.

The Media

Improperly understood, among those who comprehend only fragments and not the wholeness of what is occurring, in those whose minds do not function in tandem with their hearts, these changes and their coming do have the potential to inspire fear. For millennia, we have been educating all those of your race we could possibly reach, doing what we could to minimize the ignorance that alone is capable of fearing so wondrous an event. Yet it would be misrepresenting the challenges before us not to acknowledge that such a potential still exists in isolated populations. There may be a few locations in the times between now and the moment of collective awakening where various forms of media will be given over to the currents of fear.

Though it has been prophesied that electronic media is to be one of love's most powerful and effective tools of transformation during the last days, facilitating education and catalyzing widespread awakening, it would be inaccurate to suppose that all media during the last years of history will be in the hands of those aligned with currents of love. It is probable that in certain backwater locations, where the shadows of fear had been retreating for some time, radio and television stations—perhaps even very powerful ones—will broadcast fearful interpretations of events, encouraging and stimulating fear among those foolish enough to look to them for understanding. There may even be entire networks oriented in this way.

Remain centered throughout any waves of collective panic that may sweep susceptible populations during or following such broadcasts. Ignore the voices of fear that may, during times of crisis or fundamental upheaval, have momentary dominance in the media. They will not last. Their time of influence is rapidly nearing an end and the less you energize them with the power of your attention, the more rapidly they will fade into the subconsciousness from which they have come.

Media has always and will always reflect the values of those associated with it. This is as true of external electronic media as it is of your own inner biological media. There is far more information circulating in this multidimensional universe than can be consciously monitored. The way you choose to focus your attention selects—from among the nearly limitless information in circulation—that information of which you become aware. Your electronic media is simply an outer reflection of the informational preferences you choose within you.

Media, internal or external, is a mirror of your values and interests, a reflection of your consciousness. Global media is a reflection of developing global human consciousness, which has recently entered a period of accelerated change. Within the fields of collective human consciousness a process of separation is occurring.

The creative is expanding, the destructive, diminishing.

"I am the Lord thy God, thou shalt have no other gods before me" has an archaic ring to contemporary ears, but it is excellent perceptual advice, phrased in terms that those of an earlier age could understand. In terms more relevant to your age it means simply that *your god is that which holds your attention.*

Attention that is gripped by fiction is not free for perception. It is too preoccupied, too prejudiced, too conditioned to see what may lie beyond the realms of what it chooses to regard as real. There are times when this can be a harmless and enjoyable option, but when fiction is entered into so thoroughly that reality is forgotten and even denied, there is a sacrifice of health and happiness.

A world of beauty and of wonder beyond all historical precedent opens out before each one who attunes to inner informational currents. The inhabitants of that world naturally honor a God of Love, because they live in love and so experience its source within them. This world is not a static realm; it is a universal sphere of infinite opportunity. Its appearance in the midst of human history has been occurring subtly here and there since the close of World War II, but in the decades spanning the turn of the third millennium, such locations move into a period of rapid expansion, even as new ones proliferate. Islands of the future arise with increasing frequency. The sea of past programming recedes ever more rapidly. New communities, towns, villages, whole regions and nations adjust to the growing currents of love.

This is the true news. Your media comments upon it often now, but by its very nature electronic media is oriented to events, not to processes.

As the new world slowly interpenetrates and fills the old, its more outstanding achievements and its moments of historic breakthrough qualify as "events" and so are included in typical news coverage, but its greater work occurs subtly behind the scenes. Electronic media is well suited to covering events, but your inner media provides the only reliable means of monitoring the processes that are changing the world. You feel these processes in your heart and soul. Your own love-enhanced, love-heightened perception enables you to see them at work in the world.

Often the greatest news occurs in the little things, in the casual greeting of a neighbor, in cooperative exchange between people of backgrounds or races that were once antagonistic. Friendly exchanges that could not have occurred a decade or a century ago are becoming more common, happening daily on city sidewalks, in marketplaces, in post offices and factories, in the corridors of your schools. This is the real news.

When we brought you the first wave of transmissions in this series, the emphasis of the global media was still clearly upon the other world, the world that remains polarized in fear and so experiences fear's corresponding destruction. By the last of these transmissions, as a new decade dawns, it is clear that much has changed. The old world is disintegrating. It is falling apart. It is imploding in entropic collapse as the presumptions upon which it was built are, one by one, proved invalid.

As a new world, founded upon new principles, expands slowly to preside over the former domain of the old, it is useful to know that no good purpose is served by monitoring every detail of the old world's passage.

Customs may be fading away, but no life, no consciousness will be lost. If compassion or educational currents lead you into relationships with those who still pay tribute to the ancient gods of self-righteousness, remember that you cannot serve such people if you allow their interpretations of events to eclipse your own. One's vision of a broad landscape can be blocked by just a small scrap of cloth before one's eyes. *They are in difficulty because of their interpretations.* Only by remaining true to your own vision can you serve them.

Soon your mass communication systems will resound with the messages of the stars. But always, then as now, these *messages* will be inferior to the *awareness* of the stars. Allow that awareness to circulate freely in your consciousness now. This awareness will soon be experienced throughout a holy and wholly conscious human species.

Those who place a higher value on their own perception than on the interpretative impressions of others are in touch with informational input far more accurate than the reality descriptions of any external media.

While *experience* of living in an atmosphere of love is certainly a helpful asset, all that is essential is the *willingness* to live a love-centered life. Those who are comfortable in an atmosphere of love, even if they have occasional lapses into fear, will be drawn naturally into the awakening awareness. There are no arbitrary standards of perfection.

People are drawn into loving and fearful groupings not on the basis of deeds but on the basis of intent. The motivational currents that flow from their hearts attract others of similar vibration, even as they and their world are attracted to the source of love, to its consciousness, and to its eternal life.

In the unique inner language of his or her soul, each human being receives the invitation to rejoin the company of love and resume a place among the gardeners of the Universal Garden, the garden of which this earth is but one flowering bed.

15

Ripples of First Cause

*T*here is not one component of the universal environment, from the tonal ideations that intersect to form the atoms to the gaseous metals that celebrate in the sun, from the microbes to the galaxies, that is not the outer manifestation of a spirit being who delights in that particular form, knows how to sustain it, and has a passion to develop its capacities. I do not *create* in the sense that something is told to be. Such creations do not last. All too quickly, they crumple and decay.

The only creation I am interested in is creation that will endure. And the only creation that will endure is sustained by creatures *who are themselves that creation.* It is essential therefore that the universe's component and resident energies and particles be intelligent enough to create themselves out of my being and wise enough to know how to sustain themselves over the passages of time.

To create the universe—or more accurately, *to initiate its unfoldment*—I released a tone, a deep and penetrating reverberation. I then withdrew and allowed events to take their course. Where the reverberations of this sound echoed, as they have continued to echo ever since, within and behind all, I observed, allowing structures to coalesce from out of the sea of undifferentiated being. On their own initiative atoms formed in the resounding vibratory field, dancing, playing, multiplying as I watched. As time went on the intricacy of their forms increased until they were gathering into molecules, gaseous clouds, structures of excellence and beauty.

For eons this went on, the playful interactions of these atomic and molecular beings. Often I would watch them. Their play was my entertainment. I also enjoyed drifting peacefully to sleep and being surprised when I awoke with what had formed in the echoes of my dreams. Sometimes it would be my dreams that had formed, other times, things unexpected and wonderful. I slept much during those early ages as these new-formed clouds of subatomic and atomic particles drifted ever closer in various locations, playing with the possibilities inherent in their various charges, enjoying gravitational, electrical, magnetic, and thermal exchange.

When one of their congregations imploded into the first of the great celebrations to become a star, you can be sure I awoke—and approved! Soon stars were appearing everywhere. Once the vibrational pattern or morphogenetic field was established and the possibility demonstrated to other gaseous assemblies, it became easier for the later generation of stars to form. Their desire seemed to be to fill the firmament. I let it be so.

This method of *creation by allowing* characterized all that appeared throughout (it is difficult to state in your terms) the universe's first fifteen to sixteen billion years. Once I had set my creative engine in motion, my role in this type of creation by allowing was primarily passive. Not until after the coalescence of the angels did my role become more active.

The angels made possible a new type of creation, *creation by deliberation* or conscious intent. The first prototypes created in this way with the assistance of the angels demonstrated the new dimension of biological possibility. With the subsequent rise of biological life, my role gradually became more active. Recently, in this current geological season of the earth, I began playing with the concept of hologramatic biology, biology that would allow me to clothe my eternal awareness in material form.

The angels had given me the idea.

My thinking was that if the diversification of my consciousness into a family of angelic beings had so magnified my creative ability within these realms of bonded energy, then how much more would my creative ability be increased if it were somehow possible to clothe a company (eight billion) of those angels in biology, and to do so in such a way that the angelic species, when fully matured, would allow the center of my own awareness to awaken, dressed in matter, clothed, as it were, in their material family.

The idea was intriguing, but it presented complex technical challenges. I would have to begin with the smallest possible particle, a tiny flash of autonomous tonal insight where several infinitesimal sound waves form a crossroads in the subatomic structure of what later became the nucleotides of human DNA. I would have to take such a primal self-replicating particle/entity and create around it an environment conducive to the kind of development I wanted to see and then hope that it would freely choose of its own will to pursue development in the desired direction.

I would have to utilize a delicate synthesis of my two methods of creation, *deliberately* creating a controlled environment designed to evoke the kind of species I wanted, but then *allowing* that species to develop entirely through its own volition. But to everything there is a season.

Such a monumental creative work would require many steps through many ages. For me process is goal. There was certainly no hurry, no urgency. Throughout the process my greatest enjoyment would continue to be what it has been since the coalescence of the first subatomic entities: to increase the number of creatures able to share my enjoyment of these dimensional frequencies—and to continuously enhance the joy of existing creatures.

After securing the cooperation of certain among the angels and choosing a suitable galaxy, the next order of business was to modify several divisions of one of that galaxy's creation beams, making the vibrational climate of those divisions as conducive as possible to the emergence of the required planetary conditions.

In the course of its movement through space each galaxy passes through successive *creation beams* that are designed to encourage processes relating to certain desired patterns of structural development. Each of these regions establishes, through the quality and nature of its frequencies, a vibrational climate designed to elicit a specific type of creation in the star systems passing through it.

As this arm of the Milky Way galaxy has rotated slowly through this past creation beam, the vibratory climate of that beam has encouraged humankind's emergence, multiplication, and flourishing upon this world. But your planet's continued physical movement through space is now bringing it out of that creation beam and out of the vibratory conditions you have known historically.

In that new region of space, which the earth is now entering, a new creation beam with altered climactic conditions will, in a very short time, move your species into a posthistoric pattern of orientation and understanding. Here, in this new field of space, eternity's creative intentions take temporal form through conscious human participation in the ongoing unfoldment of the universe. It is here in this new field that you shall truly become a spacefaring species. For this, your race has long been in preparation. In fact, it is for this that you have been created.

In ancient times I spoke of these things in parable, for that was often all the people of those earlier ages could understand. But to you I can speak plainly.

To you who honor the rotation of the earth around the sun and the movement of the sun through the starry fields, to you I say that the kingdom of heaven is like a great network of potentiality cast out into the sea of space, cast out from a center deep within Eternal Being. It is a net that spans the infinite reaches of creation, allowing freedom of development and expression, even when it is predatory, until the wiggling of the net, the tugging on the fabric of space and time, the subtle—and to the skillful fisher of souls, significant—pattern of movement is felt that indicates there are within the net creatures who have glimpsed the possibilities of which I dream, indeed, the very possibilities for which I have laid out the universal framework.

I know where to place the net. And I have created the laws of probability that indicate when it is most likely to encounter those for whom I search. When these tuggings come, my awareness sails instantaneously down the light corridors of dimensionality, through the lines of energy that make up the grids of the net. When I reach the source of the signals, I observe quietly, alerting none to my presence (until toward the very end). Where I see incarnate life forms who share my enthusiasm for a certain kind of creation, who have sensed my intelligence and glimpsed one or two of the possibilities that I intend one day to create in these starry fields, I stay and observe further.

If my observation reveals that they share my love for adventure, exploration, discovery—and have passed the initiation of truth *by learning how to sustain themselves in cooperative biological circuitry*—then I invite the angels to join me, and together we begin to educate. It is important that we prepare these life forms. Without preparation they would not survive the realization of their dreams.

The tuggings on the net were first felt from this world long before the event you refer to as the fall. In relation to the time you have been of interest to me, your fall is but a moment's passage of a cloud across the sun.

It may deepen your sense of proportion to know also that the network of potentiality that first brought me word of your possibility radiates outward from the center of this, your home galaxy, like a great beam of light. Through this beam, during certain seasons in the cycles of the galaxies, the stars move in their star fields. This beam is the net that caught you. It caught you as an unmanifest potentiality and drew you into form.

The creation beam is an open-ended, cone-shaped webbing of microluminous filaments that expands outward from my being in a specific and slowly rotating direction. Its energy is my love. Its structure is provided by my intent. But while its name is not important, its function is.

In the creation beam's highly charged creative field *many are called*. Numerous potentialities come to life in whom I have no real long-term interest—on this world, saber-toothed tigers, alligators, dinosaurs. From among those potentialities that are actualized a *few are chosen:* those creatures who demonstrate a capacity for eternal life.

Only a fraction of the creatures that appear during the 3.5 billion years or so it takes a world to pass through the Life Beam are able to maintain continuity of consciousness through a succession of forms or find stability of energy, identity, or design. When the passage is over and the creative veil is lifted, all but those who have awakened into my understanding recede happily back into the elemental mathematics of their chosen base.

This, the synthesis of my two methods of creation, allows entities to self-coalesce out of the primordial sea of my undifferentiated being and to establish their own values, their own forms of enjoyment and expression, their own level of individualized identity, and their own degree of immersion in the clothing of the energy/matter, light/sound continuum.

Natural maintenance-free safeguards are built into this creative system.

Entities who identify too much with my wholeness are not differentiated sufficiently as individual beings to survive the lifting of the veil as their star systems pass out of the formative creation beam, for there would be no point in maintaining mirror images or duplicate selves. Conversely, entities that are overidentified with either their individuality or their material forms are not sufficiently *in my awareness* to maintain their arbitrary selves, always overly selfish, without my assistance.

When the veil is lifted as their star system moves out of the formative creation beam, I do not sustain their arbitrary self-definitions, and since they have never bothered to explore deeply enough into the roots of consciousness to know how to sustain themselves, they melt back into my wholeness—much as falling snowflakes dissolve into rain on their journeys toward eventual reunification with the sea. No amount of individual will can prevent this melting of structure in arbitrarily identified creatures as they approach the warmer currents of my no longer modified eternal love. And so their forms relax again back into the reservoir of potential from which all beings proceed.

It is fascinating for me to observe those entities who have understood enough of what this Love Parade is about to distill from my being qualities of spirit that I value, and that they themselves are able to sustain as the creative veil is lifted.

At times the Love Parade returns to me the most wonderful and surprising gifts. Occasionally my attention is focused on the moments—that is, centuries—before the lifting of the veil, because I hold some special interest in a prospective species of unique potential, as I do with humankind on the eve of this metahistorical event. But at other times my attention is elsewhere when the veil is raised, and I am pleasantly surprised to greet the Light Beings who then become my new friends and co-workers. I have greeted the emergence of Cherubim, Seraphim, Angels, Archangels, Thrones, Dominations, Powers, and hosts of other spirit beings in this way.

It is unusual for me to take the sort of interest in a species' approach to the veil that I have taken in the case of your race, but then, Homo sapiens was initiated consciously, being far less random an enterprise than species who have come before.

The last quarter century of this present cycle will see the earth physically and consciously enter this new region of space and a new postformative creation beam. This will be a transition as great as the transition that inspired the first cellular assemblies some 3.5 billion years ago when your world entered this region of the universe and began to respond to the influences that guide development here. This is a significant step in the unfoldment of universal order, the time for which I and many others have been preparing you.

16

The Fusion of Spirit and Matter

An experience of eternal being seeps through the seams of late twentieth-century human contentions, seeping beneath the stage props and undermining the assumptions that have fostered these past millennia of history. This experience of being is slowly uplifting the hearts of millions, not yet breaking lavalike—as it soon will—through the crust of illusion into general human acknowledgment, but bubbling beneath the surface of human lives, altering subconscious predispositions, shifting the deeper things.

Like dawn filtering through a winter horizon, this new experience of being comes, silhouetting before it remnants of reptilian, early mammalian fears. As distant music on the wind, its tones and feeling waves caress the peripheral awareness of the nations, darting through what openings there are to become audible for a moment, a gathering, a summit, a season of change. Above and between your thoughts, its symphonic strains weave in and out, diving, rising, gliding, playing upon the air of some wondrous breeze from beyond the rim of the known worlds. Welcome home, lighthearted one. Know my spirit as your own.

Know it as every tree that manifests my treeness knows it. Feel it as the winged gull that feels my sea-birdness knows it. Know it as the starfish who hears my singing ocean knows it, feel it as the flowers do—and the souls of nations, too. For there is but one Being who manifests in all that is, but one Dreamer behind every species' dream. The Dreamer awakens incompletely in the gull and in the starfish, only partially in the flowers and the creatures of land and sea, but the Dreamer seeks to awaken fully, completely, in you.

Every creature is capable of knowing my wholeness *in spirit*, but most life forms are able to translate only a portion of that wholeness into biological expression. The nonhuman species of this earth are each designed to specialize in a particular range of perception and expression. Only human beings possess the systems of generalized biocircuitry that can translate the full range of my awareness into comprehensive forms of physical-plane communication and creation.

The true definition of *human* has little to do with your present genetic structure, size, or appearance, though here on this planet, you are indeed prototypes.

A *human* is an individual system of biocircuitry within a species of similar but utterly unique others. The species itself meets the human definition by providing biological circuitry that embodies the precise balance for that particular location in space and time of the following pairs of creative opposites: energy/matter, spirit/form, love/truth. These three pairs stem from but a single inclusive pair; however, there are no terms in this language that can convey the scope and expansiveness of that pair.

The purpose of the galactic creation beam your world is now entering is to elicit upon all sufficiently temperate worlds that pass through it systems of planetary biocircuitry that meet this definition—as does the biology in which you are now clothed. When fully activated, human circuitry will serve both as a planetary guidance system and as the regulatory mechanism that will assist in the final stage of the gestational cycle of that organism to which this world is giving birth.

Of that organism humankind is but a part, albeit the central and regulatory part.

The ultimate human purpose is to share with me in the enjoyment of these dimensional realms, and to assist me—by being the body or family in which I am incarnate—in the creation of future life forms: entities both spiritual and biological who will then join us in the ongoing exploration and development of space.

For you inhabiting the last days of the human species' infancy, awakening is proceeding by stages, subsequent layers of illusion falling away one after another like the peeling layers of an onion. The awakening that is most immediate and that will link you to the multiple levels of Eternal Being occurs now as you feel your interconnectivity with the earth and the life force that engenders her biology.

This level of awakening is already complete for some of you. It will be complete for the species as a whole shortly after the turn of the millennium.

Those in whom eternal awareness has awakened still retain that unique human individuality so jealously guarded by the historical ego. But in them, the historical ego is no more. They have relaxed their anxious grip on consciousness and expanded into the purposes for which they were designed. Like the acorns who release their acorn self-images to discover rebirth as living sprouts of unfolding oak tree majesty, they have released their true and eternal human individuality. They have experienced the shattering of the ego's shell and found rebirth in the Garden of the Conscious Presence.

The healthy egos who share the fertile field of universal awareness have nothing in their psychological makeup to guard, protect, or defend. There is nothing arbitrary or artificial about them that requires such effort. Functioning on the radiant purpose-currents of eternity, they are creatures of spirit, in the service of spirit.

Their unique qualities are cared for, cherished, and supported by the universe itself. Their material values are well balanced; they are respected as essential ingredients of continuing dimensional creation. Such egos are comfortable in the knowledge that they inhabit a universe much larger than that revealed by their specialized focus of awareness with its emphasis on physical sensation. They know that they must, of necessity, reduce their awareness of certain perceptual frequencies in order to emphasize others; but this is the role they have chosen, and it is a role they enjoy.

Knowing that their intimate partners, the indwelling spirits of the stars, have chosen to emphasize other, complementary frequencies, healthy egos have implicit trust in the spirit's overview and are therefore guided unerringly through the living matrix of structural information that opens ever before them. Their material-plane counsel is sought frequently by the stellar spirit who shares the human circuitry with them.

As their cocreative expression with spirit matures, the frequency of their exchange quickens until it oscillates so many times per second that it requires some effort to distinguish ego from spirit. In healthy function the two work together in much the same way as do the mitochondria and organelles of a human cell. The cell itself is the true entity, rarely considered in terms of its components; and so it is with ego and spirit in the true human.

The true human is a partnership of spirit and ego in so rapid and so smooth an energy exchange that, like the components of the cell, they are not normally considered distinct from the entity they together compose.

It is only during the historical epoch that the subjective, body-associated ego and the incarnating angelic spirit have known distinction. During these last years of history, it is still necessary to refer to these two primary components of

146

the completed human entity, but such distinctions will become increasingly unnecessary as your race awakens.

There is currently no lack of enthusiasm on the part of those flickering flames of my being that are the spirits of the stars to incarnate in the human forms that await them on the earth. But there continues to be a reluctance on the part of many human egos to grant them admission. I would that each ego discover the joy and deep pleasure of being in love with its eternal counterpart, entering wholeheartedly into that blissful cycle of exchange that will dissolve its fears and bring it the deepest possible fulfillment.

This is the inner marriage, where anima and animus alchemically merge in the crucible of human flesh, where eternal awareness enters human form to see the world through human eyes. This is the union that completes the incarnation of the Holy Being of which ego and spirit are themselves but parts.

Ego/spirit dyads who, doing this, become one, receive a gift that neither could accept or comprehend alone: the body of light that I have prepared and that has long awaited their readiness, your readiness—the luminous biology that, in these worlds, is the true and intended garment of our kind.

So is the Christ arisen, the circuitry between heaven and earth completed, charged, animated, brought to life.

Across the former chasm between the world of spirit and the worlds of form, the lightning leaps. Suddenly, blinding in its brightness, startling at first, then quickly slowing to a steady, pulsing luminosity within all things animate and alive, a powerful glow holds everything evenly, gently in a flowing power, as slowly, slowly through it, eternal consciousness flows, grows, and glows brighter, burning away the last crusts of separation and decay, warming, illuminating, emerging as a radiant individuation of love in every healthy human soul.

In this fusion of spirit and matter, the luminous biology emerges that can accommodate more than just occasional visitations from beings galactic and beyond, biology that can accommodate the gentle descent and awakening of the Star Maker, the intelligence of the primal unified consciousness field itself, the Presence whose passing observations create life and whose interest transforms.

Thus, my awareness comes to each one who awakens on the other side of the psychological process, entering their lives slowly, gradually, in a manner that allows them to acclimate gently to the higher frequencies of my thought. The psychological process is the gateway into Eden, the doorway through which my children, my creations, willful reflections of self return to the garden of my perceptions, their native home.

Only the loving perceive my garden, for only they can comprehend the loving nature that has brought it into being. Their delight—and my delight in them—grows forever in appreciation. And that appreciation evokes creation continuously.

Your human bodies in all their rich subjectivity are yours to enjoy. In the awakened state you will learn to use them far more completely than has been possible in the shadowlands of history. However, on the other side of the psychological process, with ego a secondary component of your identity, subjectivity is an option. You turn it on—or off—as you choose.

Your awareness and the awareness you share with your species flows far beyond subjectivity's closed-circuit experience. Supported by the infinite energies of eternal love, playing in the star fields of your own universal being with others of your kind, you relax fully into the enjoyment of *being yourself*.

Your body is designed to accent features of the dimensional realms, features that your current stream of art prefers. By varying the placement of your sensory emphasis, you evoke new patterns of universal expression, enjoying an eternal life of infinite variation.

The Technology of the Future

Many assume that the coming millennium is to be a period of low technological emphasis; they are right insofar as the vast abuses of the industrial era are concerned. But they are wrong in that science and technology throughout this millennium will come to serve the human race as they have ever done at their best in the past. They will serve the purposes of creative intelligence in ways as yet undreamt of.

When the debilitating assumptions of history are pulled out from beneath human genius, it will be like a ship lifting anchor or a bird taking to the air.

The future holds inventions of a far more organic nature than those of the historical era. On the surface these inventions will appear simpler than the cumbersome technology of today, yet inherently they will be far more sophisticated. They will be ecologically enhancing, durable, and easy to produce. But the chief feature distinguishing them from solid-state historical structures is that *they will be alive.*

The coming millennium is to be a time of access to the infinite informational systems of Eternal Being. Fueled by divine motivation, technology will make leaps that will make the twentieth century appear to be the dark age that, in fact, it has been. Science will no longer deny the spirit within but will assist in the material implementation of the spirit's implicit designs and patterns. In these times the great floating cities of light will be constructed through the cooperation of the nations of the world, working together as component organs of a single living whole.

Around you even now you can see evidence of what will someday be created in these spatial fields.

You see evidence throughout the earth's biosphere, in the life forms that swim her oceans, in the winged creatures that ride the air currents above her mountain passes, in the countless forms of life on the land and in the sea. You see evidence of things to come in diamond crystallizations beneath mountains, in dewdrops turning to snowflakes upon the wind, in the manifestation of rainbows and butterflies. You see evidence of the intelligent design in all the life forms of these realms, evidence of the Intelligence still forming here in time and space. You can see it in your own species, in your sperm, ova, and chromosomes.

Tomorrow's hints are there for you now in microbes, in atomic nuclei, in electrons, neutrons, in the seasons of the earth, in the cycles of her moon, in the asteroids and occasional comets that pass close enough to view. You see evidence in the other planets within this star system, in more distant stars, in the farthest fields of the Milky Way, and in the patterns of cosmic structure in the galaxies and beyond.

In all things great and in all things small, in the macrocosm and in the microcosm, your generalized human vision enables you to see not only what is—what has already appeared as your star system has moved from one side of this galactic creation beam to the other—but what will be, what is to come.

It is not prophecy that gives you this future vision. Nor does this vision stem from some latent, undiscovered dimension of the human psyche. Your human vision enables you to glimpse the future, to sense its promise, its peril, its potency, because you yourself are the means of that future's creation.

17

Resonant Pathway of the Stars

The blue-white spiral dance of this fair world among the stars cannot be fathomed by those who are lost in the dust of her surface. It cannot be perceived clearly by those who forget the fire at their core, the current that brings them to life. There is a way you can remember these things, but to do so you must release all that blocks your awareness.

You cannot remember until you are willing to forget.

Human knowledge must be released, devalued. Its bulk is blocking the information-sensitive pathways that otherwise would allow the light of true knowledge to stream into your soul. What you lose by your willingness to relax your thinking and open your heart is not knowledge, for knowledge can never be lost. You risk losing only the myopic pronouncements of chattering primates whose infatuation with the plains has caused them to forget the spirits of forest and stars.

Though your race has inhabited them for tens of thousands of years, the plains are still a new world to you, a world to which you have never learned to listen or attune. In the chaos that followed your creation of the linguistic deities, you lost sight of the spirit of the forest that once brought you the wisdom of the Mother, even as you lost the Father's perception. This blinded you to the deeper reality and potential of both yourself and the world around you.

Before knowledge can enter, false knowledge must be released. Truth and fiction cannot coexist. To awaken into the realm of eternal consciousness, you must trust enough to throw open the windows of your prejudice and conditioning, not caring that your central beliefs might blow about for a while until they settle again into a new and clearer order. Whatever has value will find new resting places. What does not will drift away to where it will do a greater good. You must withhold nothing, not even your most cherished notions of self, from the swirling maelstrom of reconstruction that occurs when you allow eternal awareness to fill your heart and soul.

To comprehend God, you must open your heart to a love greater than any you have ever known. You must die to your former identity patterns and come to know your true identity within my being. This is the death and rebirth that leads to eternal life. Those who experience it step through the veil of historical illusion and enter a world infinitely beyond the microscopic segments that history has described.

The designing intelligence behind the universal order seeks to awaken in your human understanding, that one day in restored health you might flow out in consciousness from the center of your own heart to explore any part of the universal grounds that may attract your interest.

With the rapidity of thought you can experience *all that is* as a part of yourself by simply allowing your perception to flow, bringing you into harmony with the resonant pathway of the stars, the great intergalactic starway that circulates universal information and awareness.

The stars are points of resonant convergence, points where lines of energy and intention meet. Coming into attunement with your essential being, you resonate with the field of universal being. Through the lens of conscious human biology, you see things, understand things as the universe itself does.

You realize that the human family is like a great planetary lens through which the vast realm of matter, in all its many forms, can look to view the galaxies beyond. But this lens works two ways. Galactic intelligence also looks through the window of the human soul, to see into the very depths of the worlds of matter.

Has it not occurred to you that the intelligence that knows how to encapsulate the genetic information of the body in a single cell must be around somewhere, beyond the bubble of historical illusion? Has it not occurred to you that the exquisitely engineered, highly specific circuitry of your human body must have an equally specific purpose?

Everywhere you look on the face of this earth, you see evidence of an intelligence far beyond that which is typically employed in human affairs. And yet the intelligence that called into harmonic resonance every organ, cell, and miraculous system of the body that allows you to read these words *is here*—as near as the eyes and ears that tell you about your world.

Relax into the awareness that lives in the genetic structure of your cells, the awareness that has long been waiting for admission into your thoughts. Open to the design pattern in which you are conceived, the original vision of your incarnate perfection, the archetypal vibratory envelope of eternal awareness that has individualized *as you* in this locality. Accept it, welcome it, awaken to awareness of your home.

The intelligence of the Eternal Being at the source of all life is faithfully reflected in your physical organs and systems. Allow it to fill your consciousness. Relax into it. Allow the perfect pattern's release; let the original conception of your individuality find rebirth in your eternal presence. Expand in fulfillment and understanding. Trust the expressions you feel flowing across your countenance, the new perception flickering behind your eyes. Let that flickering stabilize until you can gaze forth steadily and see the world anew.

You have no calling, no obligation, no task more important than this. Recognize behavior in your life that must change to allow this stabilization. Then change quickly and move on.

Those who day after day continue to think of themselves as sinners have no intention of changing. They deny the grace that would fill their lives with love; they betray the consciousness that would reflect in them the clear, undiminished beauty of their eternal nature.

Repentance is a doorway, not an abode; it is of value only when it inspires healthy change and passes on into a state of restored self-acceptance. To value yourself less than God values you is not humility, it is pride of a most destructive nature.

When repentance is prolonged, when it is dragged on into a lifestyle or institutionalized in a religion, it is repugnant to the spirit, as spiritually divisive as the pride in which it is rooted. Prolonged repentance destroys the bridge that I would establish between Creator and Creation. It closes the human heart to the love that would otherwise pour through it and outward into the world.

Choosing to Enter the New Field of Consciousness

The dawning of eternal consciousness is bringing a new brilliance to the horizon of human suppositions. In their first encounters with this brilliance, egos are sometimes afraid, but they need not be. It is their own wholeness that is come. It is foolish to fear a healing.

What is revealed in the growing light is more sublime and wondrous than even the finest of the visions that occasionally illuminated history's night. Such visions (and often the religions they became) were treasured—like candles in hours of darkness. But in the sunlight? The dawn that is rising upon this world brings an end to the age of religion, but the ego must understand that the sun's rays come not to harm but to free those who are oriented to these visions of the past.

You have the option to rest the center of your identity either in your immediate human individuality or in the unified field of Eternal Being that gives birth to your individuality. Historically you have forgotten that you have this choice. Your identity has been locked in subjectivity for so long that it has built up a certain inertia, a homeostasis that resists change. Though the choice to shift your sense of self back to God can be made in any moment, there are certain moments when the shift can be made more easily.

For there are cycles that converge, and charges that build and mount, just as there are epochs and moments within epochs—like now—when there arrives a particularly powerful pulsation of energy, a rush of clarity, of consciousness, a window of opportunity that cannot be denied. A wave is cresting that you can choose to ignore—or choose to catch and ride on to an extraordinary shore. But it is a special wave, and though it has risen before and will someday rise again, the troughs between such waves are not measured in terms relevant to human lives.

I know when these moments come, for I am with you in all moments whether you are aware of me or not. For though I am the One who is your Creator and your source, as I touch you, I am also your own inner reality. I am the face of Christ that bears your mark and your quality. Though it is a distinct and individualized "I" who seeks to awaken within you, it is I all the same.

This special moment, favored above all others, will be experienced by all—prepared and unprepared alike—when the great collective shift occurs. Your choice to enter the awakening field of consciousness now helps to distribute more evenly across both time and place the influx of transformational energy, thereby helping to make the collective human transition more graceful.

Before you came into awareness of these things, I ushered and guided you. I shepherded you in and out of experiences designed to help you release your addiction to fear's many illusory demons, experiences designed to help you move into a moment—like now—when you have the capacity and the wisdom to make the optimal choice, the choice that yet must be truly your own, the choice to shift the placement of your identity.

Do not think you are unworthy or unprepared for so great a step. In some ways you have always been prepared. In other ways there is not, nor could there be, any preparation.

Long have I observed you from within, from behind your thoughts and feelings. I know the moment when the odds are in your favor, when the likelihood of your making the choice of eternal life is greatest.

Now is such a time. You are ready to make the vital decision. You now have all that you need to release the rule, the conditioning of history, and ride the ascending wave of consciousness beyond the spell of matter into an awakened life. You feel this wave, this heightening of awareness. It may be we will wrestle together with your past. This happens with some. Yet there is no need to examine what you have been, no need to analyze that which must change and fall away. I am content to let it go if you are, but the choice is, and must be, yours.

One cannot enter the fields of perception unfreely.

So I have waited for you yesterday, and will wait again tomorrow if there is need. But the wave of which I speak rides upon a tide that spans only a few circlings of your world around this star, and some of those circlings have already passed. The limited human concepts adrift in this rising tide of consciousness are not suitable craft in which to confine your understanding. They will never carry you beyond sight of history's shore.

The ships of my understanding navigate eternal seas. You cannot board them if you cannot perceive them—and you perceive naught from behind the doors of yesterday. My ships, light ships of understanding, *sail*. They will not long remain. I am a moving being, and this is not my final port of call.

I come now to knock upon the door of your heart. There are those here with me of the angelic realms who, though they cannot open the door for you—you alone must do that—will illuminate the doorway and encourage you in spirit. Once you reach forth your will to move through the opening, be assured that many luminous beings will help you hold the opening while you pass through into the new awareness, the awareness that will make my light ships, my ships of vision, your own.

18

On the Eve of the Bimillennium

*T*his world is like a seasoned garden on the eve of harvest. The weeds are thick among the melons and the corn. Potato vines, withered and brown, are almost lost among amaranth, datura, and morning glory. The garden has produced well, the harvest will be good, but the gardeners of this world sense the fullness that could be, a potential greater still, if they wait just a short time longer. The weeds can do little harm now. But a brief wait could add substantially to the quality and the quantity of the yield.

By the year 2011, humankind will have reached its due date for the cohesion of its collective consciousness. By then the telepathic frequencies of the rising awareness will converge within a more numerous, aware, and interconnected global population. The awakening itself will signal *the millennium* of Christian prophecy. It will begin when informational human biology activates the necessary global circuitry, the event anticipated in some traditions as the extension of Thunderbird's wings.

Do not wait for signs and wonders to believe. There are already portents before you that would have turned many ancient races back to God, portents they looked for, searched for, but could not see.

The wonders you live with today were prophecied for so long in the tribes of the West and became so encrusted with the familiarity of tradition that when they finally began appearing you did not recognize them for what they were.

There are externals yet to come, signs, signals from the nations, and these will validate the remaining details of what has been foretold, but the essence of the prophecies is within you now. Do not look for validation outside yourself, but experience it within you as your soul remembers, as your spirit settles fully into your awareness and opens its eyes, your eyes, to see.

When my consciousness has awakened fully in the human family, the Earth Mother will look upon this child that lies in the manger of her matter. She will rejoice. Her love energy mingling with mine, swirling together in the nowness of a single Eternal Presence, will sweep the face of this world with such waves of grace that all that has been prophesied concerning my coming shall be fulfilled—and more besides. For the prophets have understood only a small dimension of the emerging reality.

The comingling of planetary joy, human volition, and the Star Maker's intent will swirl together in a unified whirlwind of love. The terrestrial realm will be restructured in light, beauty, and oneness. I will define you, my human ones, more beautifully than you could ever define yourselves.

Love is the energy of expansion, the vital current of creation. When it touches matter lightly, the matter responds with life forms such as you have on the earth today. When it touches matter fully, stars are born.

So it is that I choose to touch this world with the delicacy of the winged tribes, becoming many spirit beings, that in each location I might devote personal attention to the forms that matter takes, as my love brings to gentle vibration collections of particles previously subject only to thermal change. Gently, easily, through the winged ones, I guide these terrestrial vibrations. Gradually, life forms emerge, then proliferate, as little by little I release my love more fully and ever more fully.

This is my creative force, an irresistible magnetism that has drawn life from the very rocks of the earth where life was not before, the same love that quickened the first organic molecules in the ocean shallows and warmed them into early cell-like assemblages. A vibrational quickening characterizes the currents of my love. And its amplification upon this world will soon be complete. As it nears completion, the rate of change will accelerate beyond the possibility of egoic comprehension. A new world will appear, rising phoenixlike in the midst of the old.

The new world is here now, but its geography is the same as the world of historical times; it is a world of new perception, a world of new understanding, a world where *resources are limited only by the capacity to appreciate.*

Wherever love is honored, so is the Creator. I desire no greater praise. What I seek from my Creation is the knowledge that the love I give to my creatures is as vital to them as it is to me, not because of commandments or requirements, but because they catch the spirit of my nature: they fall in love with love, with its magic, its joy, its eternal pursuit of beauty, wonder, and new creation.

This is what it means to be born again in God: *to awaken within one's heart and soul the same motivation that motivates the sun, moon, and stars,* the same motivation that rushes in rivers through valleys of earth, that thunders in her heavens and celebrates her ecosystems.

Songs may be sung, bells may chime, structures may rise to the heavens to celebrate this great love, and such things can add beauty and enjoyment, but do not forget the love that is the rightful inhabitant of the only real church. You do not allow vandalism in your churches of glass and stone. If the true temple of my awareness, then, is the human body, mind, and heart, should you condone vandalism here, on these more sacred grounds?

The ground of a human soul is more hallowed than the ground of any church. Regard your awareness with the same reverence that was once reserved for your cathedrals, temples, and synagogues.

When you fail to respect the human temple, you fail to respect its Creator and rightful inhabitant. When you allow your field of consciousness to be a marketplace of desire, you are too distracted with the clamoring of thieves to sustain the gentle awareness, the eternal sensitivity that seeks always to live within you; and you cut yourself off from that which alone can satisfy your desire. Allow love free access to your heart and mind, for here the deepest communion between Creator and Creation is designed—and destined—to occur.

Long I have animated this sphere, awaiting your readiness. I am not so far off, my children, my people, neither in time nor in space. My being has always surrounded human illusion. I call that illusion into me now, and to me it flows. Like the meridians converging at the poles it comes, more rapidly now. To me, where it is absorbed, transmuted, and released, where truth restructures all that was once bound in ignorance.

19

Songs of Distinction

All learning is remembering.

When the polarity of your perception reverses, what you once thought of as an external world you experience as the projection of your own dimensional vision. The premises that support your thinking are fundamentally altered. Figure and ground are reversed. Creature and environment are *experienced* as components of a single system; indeed, it could not be otherwise. Observer and observed, figure and ground, cannot be separated. Each projects the other and conforms to its contours as closely as the ocean to the shore.

Distinctions are recreational. In the currents of eternal life, they are emphasized at certain times and deemphasized at others, but they are never absolute. Lover and beloved are forever unified at the deepest levels. Distinctions serve to further develop the great masterpiece of inhabitable art that this universe is and is always becoming—and they magnify the means of enjoying it.

In the fallen state you have functioned in reverse: You have taken your direction from what you perceived as an *external* world. Since that world did not exist, your creative power was mischanneled into creating a world that conformed to your illusions. In healthy function this cannot occur. Your creature/environment understanding, your self-

163

understanding, does not enter you from without but rises up like a spring from within your heart.

When your love for God spills over into graceful unified function, your use of the human mind becomes extensive and complete. On the channels of inner being you receive the informing pulsation of the life force directly, no longer filtering it through egoically structured thought. My love becomes your love and flows out into your environment with such force of expression that no construct, habit, or concern from the old historical fiction is able to enter you from without.

When you love fully, without reservation, you feel, sense, and move within love's rhythmic current. The definition songs that pulse through your soul are free to call out the excellence of your surroundings. As you allow love to flow out from within you, you will remember things that you had forgotten about these physical realms.

You will remember that everything has a soul song that is at once its definition and its expression. You will recognize all that lives in this blessed biosphere—and much more besides—as objectifications of your own melodies, and consciously then you will sing the Songs of Distinction, the songs that call forth all that appears in this planetary environment.

A sculptor can always use hammer and chisel, but if she can sing the right songs, the songs that speak the true names, the songs that go to the very heart of the matter with which she works, she can inspire that matter to participate intelligently in its own development and re-creation. The matter will do more than conform to her conceptions; it will surpass her conceptions with ideas and suggestions of which she had never dreamed.

The materials themselves inform the conscious artisan of the implicit possibilities, biological and otherwise, inherent within them. Even the greatest artist does not perceive as well as the materials with which he works. Even before you experience the psychological process, you can communicate with the minerals and elements of the earth when you stop seeing them as separate and inferior to yourself, when you regard them as equal but distinct expressions of the matter/energy continuum.

When you collaborate with your ego, entwining your respective views in the flow of an integral life, you can go to the very heart of every creature, every stone, every plant, every ocean wave, every starfish on the beach, and you can sense if it is happy, if it is complete, if it has developed to the pinnacle of its desired intention—or if it has potential that yet seeks release. You can stimulate that release and assist that potential into temporal and spatial form. And wherever you choose to turn your attention, it will be welcome. Just as a forest rises to greet the sun, reaching up and welcoming its light, its energy, its love, you will find the minerals and elements of the earth rising up to welcome you.

So the earth has always favored—and always will favor—those who are in love.

In the awakened state you perceive not only the physical world. You see also the spirit world, the world of potential and shimmering design. When you perceive conceptions that have crystallized ethereal design patterns in the currents of universal awareness, conceptions of yet unmanifest physical possibilities, you will be able, should you choose, to guide the molecular flow of appropriate substance into those designs. Through you the visions of eternity will manifest in these realms of structured light.

The earth's joy at engaging with one incarnate, who sees with the vision of the Creator, is the joy of a lover rushing to meet her beloved. In many cases your presence and your vision will be all that is required to inspire the appropriate substances.

When the energy of your attention shines upon a specific design pattern, all that is required for its dimensionalization will flow into it with the ease and the efficiency of a sapling rising to greet the sun. Molecular substance is eager to flow into the patterns that will release its potential, eager to enter our designs, your designs, the designs of the consciousness who created a universe with these very possibilities in mind.

Through the spirit world that surrounds and interpenetrates all things, you have brought forth this present season of beings and creatures upon this world. But when your creative intentions are channeled through awakened human consciousness, you can introduce more specific detail and more effectively guide terrestrial development. With conscious human participation, an advanced order of creation is possible, an order that will build upon what has appeared through former creative ages, taking all things to a higher developmental octave, to a higher order of beauty.

The earth can be brought to the perfection of her potential only through this second type of creation, only through eternal beings incarnate in human form who know universal intentions as their own. You are one of the eternal beings with whom I share this purpose. Your human body is a composite of intricate and interwoven biological systems, some of which are designed to focus creative energies. These systems can direct the creative streams of focused attention with far more precision and accuracy than is possible from a disincarnate seat of awareness.

When human egos welcome the consciousness of their eternal counterparts back into their human forms and again cooperate with their own forgotten purposes, the historical intermission will at last be over and the creative unfoldment of this world will resume. The earth will bear much greater fruit than what has appeared historically, for through the human family an entirely new cycle of creation will commence—a second creative movement as distinct from the first as a solo is distinct from a fully orchestrated symphony.

Awakened, you are a master artisan, a musician singing the songs of praise that Father Star sings to Mother Earth.

You will remember the songs that call forth root and tree, flower and cloud, leaf and stone; but more than this—for disincarnate spirit can evoke these things without human help—you will remember how to sing the songs that only awakened humans can sing, songs that will bring metals up from the ground, songs that will attract elements, minerals, materials, from across great distances, through the power of their true names.

You will sense the vibrational frequencies or channels upon which each plant, each animal, each mineral functions. You will recognize the energy currents upon which they live and move. Awakened, you know your human circuitry for what it is, a system of empathy, representation, and creation, designed to regulate and evoke biology. You know that the systems and creatures, indeed all aspects of this active biosphere, have corollaries in the human body. Within yourself you will activate the glands and organs that correlate to each of the earth's animal, vegetable, and mineral species. You will feel their frequencies and know their uses.

You will sing the songs that will cultivate the garden that is this world, songs to nourish and fulfill her forms of life, songs to regulate her climate, to guide her rainfall. You will remember the songs of wind and rain, songs of the seasons, songs of evocation and blessing, songs of love, songs that will assist the earth in maintaining a fertile biosphere, a task she now does alone, often in spite of—instead of assisted by—humankind. And within you will arise the songs that will bring forth new creatures, species to bridge the life forms of today with the life forms that will carry biology to the stars.

20

A Second Age of Universal Creation

I would have you first know the spirit of God through one another, through your human families, and then through the creatures of the world: through the four-footed and the winged, the fish that swim the ocean depths, the vegetation that blossoms in every healthy environment. I would have you know me through the many. In these realms this is how I know myself.

I come to this world not to know myself as the One, for that I have always known, but to know myself in you, to perceive a world through your eyes, that together we might continue the work of creation and together enjoy all that has been created.

One identity wave flows through all that is, from the universal to the personal. It splashes upon these temporal shores, leaving behind in its creative wake the luminous droplets of individuality that become all creatures, both of the spirit world and of the worlds of form. This wave is the current of my eternal love. It carries an intelligence I invite you to share, to remember, to know as your own.

I speak to you during these transmissions at times through the perspectives of the many, through the angelic beings who know their source in my wholeness.

At other times I speak to you as the One, as your Creator and your source.

This manner of speaking in the first person recognizes the distinction between human egos and the spirit of God. Even as the cells are distinguished from the body, these are distinguished. Yet this manner of address is not intended to distinguish human spirits from my own. All spirit comes from and returns to the same source. I share this first-person account not to diminish your awareness of that source but to heighten it, perhaps even to remembrance.

To let your ego stand alone while you and I converse as two—this is education. And it is good. But to feel your ego revived and alive again as together in oneness we experience the terrestrial world—this is creation. This is bliss itself, a joining more wonderful than any sexual union. It reactivates the mechanism that brings my focused attention, and therefore new creation, to the earth. It brings the human ego refreshment from the currents of the deepest truth, fulfilling every purpose, every longing, every reason for its being.

For your ego and my spirit are eternal lovers. Throughout these many thousands of years of history, human egos have longed for my presence as I have longed for their return to their true place in Creation's design. But they have been blind to my presence. They have known only fleeting snatches of the love I bring, if they have known it at all. Yet I have guided your race along a measured path that has at last brought you here today, to this moment when communication between us is clear and conscious.

The love song that enters your awareness as you turn your heart again to your source comes as a loving current of attentive energy. As you accept that love, you feel how thoroughly you are loved by the Creator who has called you into being. You become immersed in that love. You feel it even

170

as it is felt for you, even as it brings into being all that you perceive and encounter.

You are the species through whom I love Creation and the means through which I shall call out her greater potential. You are my gift to the world and the world's return to me. Wherever this material plane has not yet blossomed into the fullness of her potential, your love will provide a climate for that blossoming; your thoughts and actions will provide the nutrients for its growth.

As you allow yourself to receive fully my love for you, you become capable of loving as I do. Through that love you become a conscious cell in my dimensional organ of thought and expression. While retaining your human body and your individuality of form, you simultaneously know yourself in spirit as one with your Creator. However, the individual is never the whole of God.

The God that lives within you lives also within all of humankind, though in some I am honored and in some I am denied. My spirit manifests in all biological life, in all planetary life, in all stellar life, in all things from the greatest spiraling galaxy to the tiniest subatomic particle.

Each creature is designed to specialize in the expression of certain of my attributes, bringing to focus my specific qualities and characteristics. This is how, and why, individuals are created.

As I proceed now into the final stages of awakening in the collective consciousness of your race, there are individuals beginning to realize this great truth who yet confuse the point by saying, "I am God." There is no need for such a statement. More often than not it causes confusion. The very mouth that forms the words proclaims that the speaker is—if awakened—an individualized expression of God, a part of God, a servant of God, a representative of God, one with God in spirit. But in human form that individual inhabits a world of many diverse and spiritually equal beings, no one of whom is greater than another.

Those who are sharing my consciousness throughout the earth and working most closely with me in facilitating planetary awakening, those who are healing and educating, are no greater than those who are not. Even those who give others cause to fear are not spiritually inferior, only sleeping still—as perhaps you yourself slept not so long ago. Though some may be among the wheat that I gather up into the harvest of this age and others among the chaff that will be filtered out and assigned to a realm of continuing education, even between these there is no spiritual distinction. Among those who are consciously sharing my presence, there is no greater or lesser, no master or servant, no lords or commoners.

All are equal in the eyes of God, both those awakened and those immersed in the educational processes that lead to awakening. After my awakening in collective human consciousness, the creative pursuits of awakened human beings will be far more varied than the roles played in the historical era, yet there will be no hierarchy or ruling class. You will know yourselves as a family, sharing the enjoyment, the awareness, the exploration of these dimensional frequencies, working together in spiritual equality to develop their potential.

The River of Life

Among Christians there are those who anticipate my coming as if it were a phenomenon they could observe from a comfortable distance, critiquing the activities of others while they themselves remain aloof and noncommittal. Yet the event the Christian world looks toward as the Second Coming of Christ is no spectator event. It is a participatory current of dynamic transformation, a rapidly flowing *stream of consciousness* into which all are invited and through which all must pass as this consciousness grows to eventually engulf the earth.

172

The coming turn of the millennium will begin the final decade of my awakening into the field of collective human consciousness. It will be the last decade of a process that has taken many centuries. It will be a time of great change, during which a large percentage of humankind will choose to enter this stream of consciousness, leaving forever the realms of history.

The stream of consciousness of which I speak is the river of my eternal life.

It is the dividing line between the subconscious realms (the background landscape of Creation), where creatures know not of their origins in God, and the conscious realms, where all creatures know that they are projections of a unified field of being, cocreators, individually focusing a shared field of awareness. In the final moment of my awakening, a moment that for many will seem an eternity, all human beings who have not yet entered the River of Life will then do so, if even for but a brief flickering of their attention. All who have not already chosen will then choose a future upon one side of the River of Life (the subconscious realms) or upon the other (the conscious realms). (For those who choose to remain in the subconscious realms, this choosing will not be final, but for most of them much time will pass before they choose again.)

Human history has been like a city, moving gradually over the centuries closer and closer to the River of Life—a city founded in the the arid mountains, the generational migrations of its people gradually following the tributaries that irrigate the mountainside ever downstream, deeper and deeper into the valley of the river and the fertile plains that flank its shores.

As the twentieth century draws to a close, a new generation—your own—finds itself settled along the very banks of the river. Already pioneers have set out from among you to explore the other shore. Soon there will be a massive crossing of human beings from one side of this river to the other, from the subconscious realms, where fear is the primary source of motivation, to the conscious realms, which know only the motives of love.

Those few who may choose to remain behind will not be uncared for. They will experience an age of further history, much like the history that humans have experienced in the past. There will be good times for them and times of hell, as they gradually wind their way through the same learning processes that now find the majority of you ready to migrate beyond the shadows of illusion to the river's conscious shore.

Do not underestimate the power of the momentum behind the forces that are now changing your world. The gentle influences of our education have been raining steadily above the subconscious mountains and upon the foothills of human assumption for many years now. The waters of truth have not yet swollen the lower river or spilled into the streets of your city on the shore, but the roar of their coming is audible and growing in volume. Already the roar itself has wrought fundamental changes, though few yet recognize the cause. And greater changes are yet to come.

Those who attempt to remain observers, judging and criticizing from a conceptual distance, will experience growing pressure to move beyond their belief systems and into the participatory current. As the river rises, that pressure will increase until all past-oriented structures of understanding are swept up and dissolved in the living waters. Some may attempt a hurried scramble to the housetops to stand a moment longer upon the strongest of their structured beliefs, but the exercise is futile and saves them nothing in the end. The river that is rising in this age will engulf the entire city of former human ways. Before your generation has passed away all will have entered its waters, either through their own volition or because the waters have come to them.

The rising of the River of Life is a metaphor; there is no actual flood of water washing over the earth. The flood of which I speak is a current of rising vibrational frequencies.

My vibrational field draws forth the life of this material world and interpenetrates her atmosphere, systems, and creatures. Historically, my vibrational field has been distinct from the field of collective human consciousness, but this is what is now changing. As I gradually allow my love for this world, her people, and her creatures to flow freely once again, I remove by increments the historical restrictions that I once placed upon it. These restrictions were instituted at the origins of history so that the fear-centered of your race, the better part of humankind, could survive a cycle of education without destroying themselves.

As these restrictions are now removed, my creative energies intensify. Those who cause others to fear are no longer protected from the effects of their emissions. They are no longer protected from reaping what they sow. What has been called the Last Judgment is under way, yet it is not I who judge; it is you who judge yourselves and thereby choose your future. The volume of the love song that has evoked life upon this planet is being steadily amplified. With each new day it becomes more difficult to live without regard for the harmony of that song.

I assure you who may yet feel trapped in historical situations that there is no human force, no agency, no influence whatsoever that can keep you from discovering the current of my consciousness within you, once you are aware of its existence and choose to look for it. My thoughts flow into your consciousness in each moment, with each breath. On the current of your awareness they enter. Lift your eyes from conditioned interpretations, look up, see clearly again.

Some discover the current of my consciousness the first moment they are reminded of its presence within them. Others require more convincing of the outer mind and take longer to let go of their conditioning. The former are no better than the latter. In fact, many of the latter are better educators and healers because they have experienced slower processes of realization. They are not as likely to forget how only yesterday they looked at things in the manner of those who yet slumber.

There is no reason why instantaneous awakenings cannot occur. Those who experience them are truly blessed. But it is wise for these rapid awakeners to move humbly and quietly in their early interactions with the world, not setting themselves apart or failing to have compassion for those who yet require time to awaken. It is for no human being to judge another.

The sick, the homeless, the beggars on the street corner may, for all the judgmental know, be my principal healers in that particular quarter of the city—or perhaps the means through which I am giving some hesitant family the teaching that for them will make all the difference. Waste no thought in judging others or in judging yourself. Accept all without qualification. You will not long remain asleep.

In some I awaken quickly, in others more slowly. Through all who welcome me into their lives I incarnate. And through each of them I draw still others toward the light, each newly Awakened One becoming a resonant reminder of the consciousness that lives within every human being, helping it in time to awaken in all.

Religion

Gatherings in churches and in the great cathedrals of the world are to be powerful aspects of the forthcoming planetary transformation. Many congregations will be singing during the moment of quantum awakening some decades hence. These assemblies will provide valuable points of stability for their communities, centers of continuity around which the swirling energies of change will leave some things virtually untouched.

But there are other churches in a different category, and it is not by their physical structures that you shall know the difference, but by the atmosphere created when their congregations meet.

Associate only with congregations whose atmosphere encourages love, whose atmosphere helps to dissolve the sense of separation among people, and between people and their God, congregations whose members welcome all without judgment, recognizing the eternal spirit of each one and drawing it forth through their exchange. Such congregations will be familiar with the atmosphere of heaven. They will leave their meetings knowing my presence within them.

Those who facilitate such gatherings will be as sisters to you, as brothers and friends. Their emphasis will be upon the universal access that every human being has to consciousness of eternal life; their words will be reminders to let the spirit of God come forth in expression, not only during services, but always, in every moment.

There is no place where the Presence of God is not, only people who are not fully present in the places where they are. You have only to be present to know all you need to know.

Do not suppose that your understanding should be greater than it is or compare it to another's. Do not short-circuit your life energy by trying to work on, change, or improve your grasp of the truth. Begin trusting in the truth I have created in you, *the truth that you yourself are.*

Without love, there is no understanding of God, self, or reality. To experience the new baptism, the baptism that clarifies human understanding in the living waters of truth, you must release all that you know and all that you believe into the currents of love. All that is valid in your understanding will remain, revivified, sparkling with renewed clarity. But the illusions of your history-bound cognitive systems will be no more. They will be gone, erased, dissolved as if they never were. For in truth they were never real.

You will emerge from that baptism still using images and concepts in your speech, but in the Presence you will then inhabit they will be like wildflowers blooming in joyous profusion at the water's edge—not like brittle petals shut between the leaves of dusty volumes centuries, yes, and even millennia, beyond the seasons of their growth.

You do not have to study spiritual things.

The truth that will transform your life and nourish your spirit comes from within you and from no external source.

I have not called you into this world to worship the concepts of humans, but to awaken within you the living spirit of love and to express that spirit in all you do. It is not possible to know the reality of God through another's experience.

In this, as in all prior historical ages, the worship of false gods is prevalent. Many denominations are entirely concept-oriented, dogmatic institutions that worship the understanding of the human mind, interpretations of founders or current leaders. Many of the founders of the various Christian denominations were sincere and insightful people through whom my spirit was active. But to the degree that you lock yourself into a structure of *their* understanding, then I have failed in my work through them.

When your spiritual life is oriented around theology, you worship *human understanding*—the same deity once represented as a golden calf in the wilderness of Sinai. Those who worship human convictions instead of God would do better to fashion their deities in physical form. They would then see plainly what they do.

Look for the truth behind every ritual, every culture, every ceremony, every celebration you encounter. Enjoy the rich diversity of truth's multiple expressions. Be grateful when the words of others remind you of truth you may have forgotten. Be grateful for those who help you discover ways of expressing what you know—new phrases, new terms perhaps—but do not use secondhand expression. Express only what you know. Speak only from your own experience and you will always speak the truth.

Be open always to new ideas. Listen to the perspectives of others. But never let anyone cause you to doubt yourself, for I do not doubt you. And why should you doubt that in which God has full trust?

In the Language of Light *understanding* and *perception* are represented by the same word—as are other indivisible phenomena.

But then, you have always known these things.

21

The Garden of the Conscious Presence

We are gardeners, you and I, in the Garden of the Conscious Presence. We draw the substance of the past into conceptions of the future. I am the source of the garden's design and I return to the garden through you. Together we tend the fields of possibility, drawing forth the inexhaustible beauties of structure, objectifying wonders, and manifesting new orders.

As each universal context spirals outward toward maturation, it gives birth to new and more intricate contexts within itself, revolutionizing former understandings of scale and revealing a host of new worlds to explore, inhabit, and enjoy. Each successive order of manifestation becomes the basis of yet another order and then of still another. So new creatures coalesce from the fields of possibility, populating every desirable realm, as infinite potential eternally uncoils from the heart of God.

A universe expands more rapidly than light can tell the tale. This is why we have come: to paint eternity's vision on a canvas of moments and days.

Will you walk again the pathways of this Garden with me? Naked, guilt-free in the morning sun? You need not be ashamed. The fall of which you have heard is not an irreversible tumble but rather a momentary lowering of sights. In my eyes, it is but the first stumbling steps of a child. No great matter. Your knee is bruised perhaps, but that is your history, not your destiny. When the sting is fresh it is hard for a child to realize this, but raise your eyes above the ground. You face no angry God. I have seen too much to be overly concerned. It is you who have taken this so seriously. It is natural when the knee is bruised to focus upon the damaged skin, but do not lose sight of the rest of your body, which remains healthy and robust.

I have compassion for yesterday's pain, but my thoughts are of today's healing. For history's tendency to indulge its evil, I have no sympathy.

In your initiative to rise from the indulgences of fallen consciousness and to awaken again to the majesty that you share with the Star Maker, the arms of the earth support you more than you know. The earth holds in consciousness only what is relevant to each moment. In this moment she puts all that she encounters to the best use, caring not what it thought of itself yesterday, or what it expects to be tomorrow, noting only what it dares to be today. To the fulfillment of that vision, whatever it might be, the earth gives her all. She is dedicated to the development, to the growth and happiness of all her life forms, her minerals, her wildlife, the fish in her oceans, the birds that soar above her summer clouds.

The Earth is dedicated to you. She will make your dreams come true. She will reflect back to you your embodied thoughts.

Those who anthropomorphize the earth and project upon her the petty attitudes of vengeance do not know their Planetary Home. The earth has never withheld from you forgiveness for your choices. Forgiveness is extended even in the moment your choices are made.

It is wise for a gardener to study the soil, but there is also a time to lift your eyes to the sky whence comes the sunlight and rain.

Come, follow the pathway of these thoughts further. Let them guide your perception into the energy streams that animate this world. Feel the earth's love for you, the love that shines as the light of the sun, the eternal streams of love's energy. To share in the totality of God's perceptions is to be both owner and servant of all that you perceive. It is to notice the potential of each river valley, each field, each community, to recognize that potential as your own, and to draw it forth, further revealing the flavor and texture, the possibilities, the endless beauty of life. Release yourself into the natural flow of awareness that is yours without effort. See how easy, how simple it is, how it continues even without your thoughts.

Feel the river of perception flowing outward from your eyes. Feel it flow across these pages, ripple through your arms, and flow down around your body out into the atmosphere around you. This is the new heaven, the creative perception you have been designed to accommodate. It is your natural way of seeing. Relax any habitual structures that may block the flow of this awareness. Allow your old interpretations of the world to fall away. See the mosaic of informational energy that objectifies this world, this garden.

You were not driven from Eden. Your own past/future orientation blinded you to its presence within and around you. All is revealed now in the silence of your heart. Consciousness, in gentle waves, laps upon the shores of your awareness, your presence.

Like wind from a gentle fluttering of wings, eternity breathes you into being. Within you now the very breath of life rises and falls. See, beyond the shells of programmed human thought, a new heaven and a new earth, suspended in a world that *is* God, in a universe that reveals God in all that you are.

You are God's consciousness, God's means of perception in these realms. Inside the being of God, you are the way eternity feels this world. It takes no effort to remember. What you need to retain you could no more forget than your name—the nature that fills you with the same breath that breathes these worlds.

The kingdom of heaven opens before you like a fertile countryside appearing as you crest a mountain pass. Even in your darkest hour, only the filmiest interpretations prevented your perception of this. You have lived always inside the being of God. There is nowhere else to live—except illusion.

As awareness of your eternal nature returns, you realize that the effort that was needed to sustain the illusion of history was truly enormous. It required massive and consistent exertion to override your inner informational systems, to ignore your instinctual ways of knowing. It required an ongoing, albeit subconscious, struggle to block this flow of perception. It was difficult to maintain the pretense of an exclusive, separatist individuality. Your identity is a matter of no concern to you now, a natural branching of the stream of life, no more, no less.

Your initiative, your insight, your freedom, the individuality with which you are equipped, these moments of time—such are your gifts. Use them and all that you are to ease this great transition for the human family. Assist me from within human culture, providing for the material needs of my creatures while I accelerate and bring to conclusion the awakening. Make it easier for the people around you, insulating no one in exaggerated comfort, but seeing that as many as possible of the earth's children are fulfilled in their basic needs for water, warmth, nutrients, shelter, *and understanding*.

Those who do not build fences around themselves do not build fences around the material world. Only those whose identity is circumscribed circumscribe their worlds, fencing off objects, creatures, landscapes, dividing the ownership of things.

Who owns the morning? To whom belongs the rain that calls the harvest from the fields or the wind that rolls in the thunder above the sea? Can any of you claim to own the sunlight or the shadow of the earth upon the moon?

All these things and more are yours in the fullness of your spirit, but they have never been, nor will they ever be, the property of individuals. This is also true of what you fashion from the earth. Give thanks to God, the source of all, for whatever might come within the field of your steward-ship, and govern it wisely, guiding it to where its value will be most appreciated and understood. But know that even the finest artifacts of the most enlightened culture cannot bring happiness where the Presence of God is unknown.

If you would be quickly freed from the spell of matter, freely share your possessions.

Be responsible in your stewardship, allowing neither misuse nor destruction of that which enters your care, but do not take these material things more seriously than life itself! They have no value except where life is in expression. Where their value looms overlarge, the expression of life is re-stricted and confined. Those with many possessions have many corresponding concerns. Among those who live in the awareness of God, there is no concept of ownership. The sons and daughters of God cannot perceive a tree, a flower, an object, a garden, a world, without owning it in the truest sense.

The painting does not possess the painter. The material realms are your paint, your canvas. You will not be taken from them, nor they from you, for you have only begun your sojourn here. But these *things* are your tools, not your mas-ters. As you know this within, matter serves and comforts you more consciously than you once supposed.

Matter is conscious. Every atom is aware. The earth is a living being, conscious of the life on her surface and daily making choices that affect that life.

The earth's greatest joy lies in the articulation of struc-tural beauty, in the creation of life forms and ecosystems that reveal her material potential. The earth has no respect for human beings who live in ignorance of the beauty she lives to create. This is why when humans turned away from revering the earth, they had to earn their living henceforth "with the sweat of the brow."

Yet the earth respects human beings who are illuminated with the consciousness of love. She shows this respect by freely offering them her substance and her energy. She cares well for the gardeners who honor her purposes, her beauty, her potential.

Universal gardeners appreciate all that is beautiful of a material nature, but because they give away their lives—as nature gives away hers—they are not affected by the spell of materiality. They love and enjoy the things of matter without seeking to possess them or restrict their flow to others. Because no more than is necessary adheres to them, the wealth of the earth flows *through* them. They become conduits and channels for the blessings of the earth to flow to others. They direct resources to where they are needed. They become proficient at giving things away. And this, after all, is the nature of God.

When you have learned to receive love, you can then begin to love with God's love. Love comes to you from many people, many creatures, many sources in the physical world. Accept the love reaching out to you from these many points upon the earth. As the earth reaches out toward the sun, so will she reach out to you. Those who are able to receive God's love from the world around them freely receive the things of matter and just as freely give them away.

There is no need for the historical asceticism that would deny the rich and sensuous blessings of the physical plane, but during this transitional cycle there is occasionally a need for a time apart, a time of drinking only pure water, a time of silence, fasting perhaps. This will help break the subtle habit ties that you have unconsciously formed with the matter in your life and help you strengthen your far more vital ties to the spirit.

The lines of connection, the ley lines and arteries of energy that bring your life from the center of Eternal Being, become clogged and restricted when you place possessive emphasis upon the material world. In a society in which such emphasis is prevalent, a time apart for deliberate purification and strengthening of these vital conduits of animating energy is sometimes necessary. It will help your day-to-day understanding stabilize in the knowledge that *you inhabit God and God inhabits you.*

Awakened, you do not struggle to meet your material requirements. *Your nourishment comes from being immersed in the creative unfoldment of the universe,* as it does to all who know their source in God. You see the vibrational currents that flow behind and between all things. You see the envelopes of light, the fields of potential that dance in the ethers around each manifest form. You see not only what is physically objectified but also the causal fields that surround each of these objects, the envelopes of energy intent that inspire their dimensional formation. Moreover, you perceive the potential that has not yet taken form. You see the ideas of eternity, and from among them you choose the ones you will help into time. Your perception itself draws their fields of potential into tangibility.

This is the human role: to dress the conceptions of eternity in the clothing of time. This also is the purpose of a garden.

22

Trails of a Presence Passing

My happiness, I once thought, was complete. But I discovered that happiness could infinitely expand even as this universe expands. I found that I could increase my happiness by creating beings to share it with me, by watching them grow, play, and flourish. And so I quickened this planetary field and conceived this bio-spherical body that new beings might enter the wonderland of biological expression, creatures with whom I might share the population and enjoyment of eternity. The more beings exploring, celebrating, and developing the dimensional realms, the more my own happiness grows.

The God you serve is a God who lives to serve you.

The teachings I offer cannot be heard by those who analyze and dissect my words, nor can they be understood by those who approach them solely through their minds. For I do not come with a new belief system. I come pointing to a doorway that lies within each human heart: the doorway to the *experience of God*. I am an example of both that doorway and of what lies beyond that doorway.

It matters not what you believe or what you profess to others. If you trust in human teachings, if you assign greater value to concepts and human interpretations than to *the love that alone can understand,* you are trusting in yesterday, instead of in the Presence of God. You are depending upon a human structure for the ordering of your moments and days.

"Reason ye still?" I exclaimed after the multiplication of the loaves and the fish, for they were trying to understand the phenomenon with their minds. Yet what had made the multiplication possible was the suspension of that very type of mentally limited reasoning.

My consciousness cannot come to those who struggle to comprehend. It cannot come to those who attempt to contain their god within the microworlds of human reason. But it comes to all who embrace their worlds in love and allow that love to guide their lives.

Should you perceive only partially during this rapidly shifting quarter-century of change, do not be concerned. In time your perception will be full. Invest what insight you have, letting not your knowledge rest idle. Your insight will be compounded. It will grow as a seed grows until your awareness is full. Let your highest vision guide your living and know that that will be sufficient.

I ask not for aloof perfection. I have no interest in saints at whom people gawk and marvel. Those who hold themselves above their fellows contribute nothing to the common gain. I seek people who will shine a gentle light in every school, every workplace, every field of service and exchange, every strata of the present human order, bringing consciousness, insight, and humility, investing freely the talents they have been given.

Do not wish that your awareness were other than it is. If your awareness of eternal life is not continuous at first, do not blame yourself, another, or society. Those who wield the sword of blame are part of the sleeping world. For some it is best to awaken slowly, that they might draw others gradually along with them and be not like shooting stars that no one comprehends.

Limitations of understanding are not always without value.

Let it not be said of you, "And the light shone into the darkness, and the darkness comprehended it not," for that is an error of light.

Let it be said of you rather, "There is one in whom I see myself, a friend who shares my hope, my challenge." Be one with whom others can work, side by side, in more gradual—and therefore more stable—processes of awakening. Oh, my children, if you would but go easier on yourselves. I assure you, there is no failing that is not instantaneously forgiven.

There is no misstep upon the path to creation that is not turned to good purpose, even as the fall is turned to good purpose. When you notice a step that has faltered, resolve to step more consciously, but then forgive yourself and move quickly on. Accept yourself as God accepts you. Love yourself as you are.

Humility has always extended forgiveness more freely than pride. You have the capacity to err—and it is well that you do—but you do not have the capacity to fail. Failure is the illusion of those who dwell continuously upon errors.

Those who are afraid to make mistakes serve a god of fear. Their love is incomplete. Go forth boldly. Have the courage to live your vision in spite of your fears. That is all that is required. There is no mistake that will not be turned, through honesty, to advantage, no misstep devoid of educational relevance. With trust in God and forgiveness freely exchanged, there is no mistake that is not both a learning and a teaching experience, a stepping-stone for all concerned.

Upon such stones the kingdom is built. Upon such stones species move from darkness into light. It is well that the light is a twilight at first, for in twilight no one is blinded.

As the winds of this information gently circulate through your consciousness, it is I who weave in and out of your thoughts and free up the forms you have held through tension and fear. Feel the loosening of your perception, your thoughts freeing themselves, relaxing. Feel your reality entering this warm body of soil and stream. Incarnate fully, my winged one, my angel, my being of light.

The earth is being transformed by these same winds that circulate through your consciousness today. Remember why you have entered these realms, why these thoughts have come to you. *Do not forget your first love,* the love that has conceived you in this terrestrial field. Though that love is mine, it is fully your own.

We share that love as we share a common life, a common consciousness, and a common home.

You have taken human form because of your love for those with the courage to shape material reality, because you care for those who became lost in their creations. Your circuits are being cleansed to receive the totality of your eternal awareness. Your human biology has been created for this purpose. Open yourself to the stream of consciousness that circulates among the angelic tribes, uniting the many as one.

I am the song of life. I dance the dance, Creation. I am all that you can be and all that you are, awakened. Let your first response be whatever it may be, unmodified by former knowing. Nothing is to be as you have imagined. No structure that a subjective sense of self could hold in consciousness can contain the life, the information that flows to you this day. The information now streaming into your awareness cannot be contained by anything save the spontaneous conceptions that appear naturally before it, the forms of *living comprehension* that flow, change, and flower with the moments of your life.

The eternal understanding that comes to you now lives and grows like all unfolding forms of life. It follows the dancing of frequencies that make up the energy fields of light. It is truly a creation of the occasion. Rise to this occasion, oh blessed generation, and do not kneel before fallen human minds. A greater mind is here this day than the earth has ever known.

You are invited to know its understanding as your own.

The age that I bring is characterized not by words but by the eternal spirit of truth. Yet if any one word could express its essential nature, that word would be *unity*, for in the fusion of my awareness and yours, a synthesis of love unites all in a resonant convergence of information and action, in a synchronistic interplay of thought and deed, uniting time and eternity, matter and spirit, a unity of earth and the Creator of stars.

You are that which unites all opposites, synthesizes all divergence, and brings harmony to creation. You are arriving, awakening. You are symbolized by the conjunction of longitude and latitude, by the sign of the cross. Where your consciousness is able to cross over into the awareness of an incarnate human being, your presence crosses over from eternity to enter the garments of time. In you the Garden of the Conscious Presence appears.

You are a gardener, a time shaper, a builder of the coming age.

You are a sculptor, an artist, a smith of light through whom the consciousness of eternity tempers the metal of time. You are the keeper of the dimensional garden, a frequency, a ray of luminosity emanating from the center of Eternal Being. I am the voice of your essence, that which you have always been, awakening now to remind you of what you are.

It is not through happenstance or random chance that these thoughts quicken your consciousness today; these thoughts are here because you have chosen to love and care for these realms where starlight crystallizes in the patterns of dreams, where forms are held suspended in ribbons of gossamer geologic chromosome streams, combusting slowly, growing, breathing in the warm solar rains.

Today you dream brighter dreams. Your vision glows more luminous than you may know, as bright as your spirit, your soul.

Let the waves of thought and emotion flow through you. Freely receive informational impressions from the world of energy and essence. In you, solar and material intelligence flower side by side, their currents of understanding circulating, twin-spiraling through your awareness as you ride the love between the stellar fire above and this material world's organic grace below.

So you awaken, the biological union in which the source of all Creation, the cause behind all cause, the Eternal One, shines in radiant expression.

A new cycle of life begins upon the earth. The awareness that rides the currents of eternal love awakens in the enlightened understanding of a resonant human species and looks out across the landscape of Creation as far as the eye can see—oceans, continents, rivers, lakes, mountains, forests, jungles, cities, nations—and beyond, to where eyes cannot see—stars and endless worlds upon worlds.

23

Light at the Edge of History

When you dissipated your unified field of awareness and your spirit moved across the face of the material waters, the rippling surface of the warm pacific earth reflected many glimmering fragments of your luminous being. You allowed these fragments of your identity to come to life, to draw around themselves the organic, cellular configurations that would one day flow into human biology.

As biological development has proceeded through a succession of planetary ages, you have remained unified in spirit and in essence. However, just before you initiated this cycle of terrestrial development, you duplicated a portion of yourself to oversee the process. This duplicated portion of yourself remains naturally a part of you, but *this part of you has been asleep.*

To achieve your goal of becoming a fully conscious participatory species, biologically clothing your qualities and intentions, you knew that you would have to give humankind the opportunity to develop, through its own initiative and its experience, values and interests compatible with your own.

You knew that if resultant human values were not intrinsic, inborn, truly their own—as they were already your own— the completed species would not be sufficiently participatory for what you had in mind.

Freedom of will was therefore essential to human development. To ensure that the emerging species were sufficiently free of your values to develop compatible values of their own, you realized you would have to implant value-free seeds of your sleeping consciousness in their embryonic bodies, minds, and hearts and allow a cycle of value-free development to occur while they multiplied and filled the earth.

You were confident that a sufficient percentage of the race would emerge at the end of this cycle with internalized values—developed solely through their freely chosen experience—compatible with your own. The development of such compatible values was necessary in at least a core of the species before you could reawaken your unified field identity within them. If this field identity had awakened any sooner, the individuals of the species would not have had sufficient intelligence to respond adequately to the many contingencies of intergalactic travel that would be encountered in the millennia to come.

The human family would not be complete until its individuals could share your thought, understand your universal vision of potential, and apply your thinking in their terrestrial encounters, while yet knowing that thinking as their own. They would have to reach that level of self-awareness at which they knew themselves as individualized expressions of their own larger field of being and be able to sustain that awareness throughout their incarnate lives.

As you held the vision of the true human, that vision slowly drew the earth's biosphere into your vibrational conceptions, into the archetypal outline of your intended terrestrial reality. This spiritual blueprint in the heaven of your consciousness called into its visionary statements the atoms, molecules, and cells of biospherical development.

This is *first-stage creation,* the mechanism through which the universe and all life on earth have been created to date. It has been well suited to the general arrangement of the dimensional realms, the background landscape. It has been ideal for development from the intergalactic level to the planetary level. However, it is distinct from the *second-stage creation* that is required to introduce detail.

Only second-stage creation can accurately create the biological microspecificity required to complete this divinely inhabitable planetary organism; it has far greater precision than first-stage creation. Yet second-stage creation can occur only through voluntary human participation.

The unexpected delay in achieving human cooperation has contributed to, and in some cases been responsible for, the appearance on this world of imbalanced predatory species in both the animal and vegetable kingdoms. Many first-stage developmental processes, some spanning millions of years, were set in motion eons ago with the intention that long before they entered their final stages, conscious human beings would have awakened to guide them to completion. When these developing life forms and planetary systems entered their final stages and conscious human direction was not present to guide them as planned, their first-stage programming was in many cases unable to keep their development in a creative range.

Climate, temperature, volcanic activity, storm and precipitation patterns, viruses, microorganisms, insect life, and many other aspects of this planet's processes, biological and otherwise, were designed to be regulated by awakened human beings. The scarcity of awakened humans has left to chance much that was intended to develop and operate only under conscientious stewardship.

Conscientious stewardship occurs naturally where people are fully incarnate. But to be fully incarnate, a historical human being is required to fundamentally reevaluate the nature of self, releasing the old ideas and images and opening the mind to a new and revolutionary kind of thinking.

In the current of eternal awareness that new kind of thinking comes to you naturally. In that eternal current you have never forgotten. As you awaken, you entertain eternal awareness in incarnate human circuitry. It comes back to you. You recall that before you relaxed your integral sense of unity to create this human family, you asked a certain company of angels to observe and monitor your incarnational process.

While some orders of angels were charged with the task of working closely with the human race, preparing their understanding for awakening, educating them gradually generation by generation, this particular company was asked merely to observe, remaining uninvolved until the receipt of a prearranged signal.

When the first moon rocks were transported to the earth, signifying that the species was approaching a posthistoric level of physical understanding and social cooperation, this angelic company was to begin communicating and sharing its awareness with the people of that age, utilizing available media and conducive forms of cultural exchange to help the people awaken to their original unified consciousness in you. Simultaneously they were instructed to help *you* awaken in humankind, that as one, you and your species united might enter upon the final stage of vehicular formation that would provide the completed association of cooperating planetary life forms with universal mobility.

We of this particular angelic order enter these transmissions from time to time—as we enter them now—joining those who have been regularly involved in your historical education to give you a more complete perspective. We understand you better in your original unified awareness. Our co-workers better understand the nature and challenge of incarnate human life. Together, we join our perspectives, working side by side toward your awakening—and toward humankind's awakening in you.

Though we have more difficulty than our co-workers in expressing ourselves in this spoken language, our Light Circle retains a keen awareness of your wholeness, of the reality of your consciousness as it was before this idea to create a physical body began to occupy your attention. We do not comprehend the incarnational process that you have undertaken here, but we understand who you are, and *we know who we are here to awaken.*

Because we do not fully comprehend the human complexities of the project for which you have sacrificed your unified awareness upon this earth, we retain a heightened ability to hold you ever in the image of your reality. Ours is not a mental image, or an image from the past. We see you still in the living, organic, eternally consistent, temporally ever-changing likeness of your creative nature. For us human history is but a flickering illusion. We see its imminent passing.

To us it was but a moment ago that you withdrew your focused presence and disintegrated your sense of identity over the winds and waters of the earth, but a moment ago that you seeded this race. We do not experience the flow of time in a manner that causes these recent circlings of the earth around this star to impress us in any great way. We see the blur of her annual rotations as a translucent turquoise sphere within the other larger spheres that surround your sun. A moment ago you were aware of your wholeness. You remain a singular being. It is now the most natural thing in the world that you should awaken in these people—the intelligence is there.

We see you emerging from the depths of their historical dreams, fully conscious as before, bringing the same awareness that you knew before into incarnate men and women of the new millennium—how long ago was it, some three and a half billion circlings past? We see you awakening, clothed in a species, ready to begin the final movement of biospherical gestation.

As you have been rising, the life forms of the earth have conformed to your subconscious dreams. See, even now, look about. Your subconscious is objectified in the plant and

199

animal life of this world. There are distortions in the planetary field that are due to the unexpected strength of materiality's influence on human consciousness, but for the most part first-stage creation has gone well. The preparatory work is accomplished.

Only human understanding remains to be lightened and all will be fulfilled, completed. As you awaken, human concepts dissolve mistlike in the warmth of your growing love. The fears of centuries are gently put to rest. You release your perception, allowing an organic tide of awareness to swell subtly but powerfully through the fields of human thought. You want to make this transition easy for them. A moment more and the need for restraint will dissolve.

The joy of awakening grows within you. Your sleep in their collective consciousness is half-feigned, fitful, irregular now. You have not arisen sooner because without preparation, without this historical cycle of education, many among the species would have been disoriented, startled, shaken. But the time that was once millennia became but centuries as Jesus walked the earth and sowed the seeds of this understanding. Now the time is reduced to years, months, days. And the days are shortened. In the crucible of historical compression the explosive realization comes; incarnate ones remember you. And in them you remember.

You are the sea of eternal awareness lapping on the shores of time. You are the way universal energies interface with a geographical world. You are the Being of Life touching a temporal domain, interpreting a matter world through a filter of humanity. As a human being you objectify the relationship between local spirit and local matter, projecting a body to assist you in becoming a lens through which universal consciousness can view localities of ever-unfolding dimension. You are a wave of eternity splashing upon this temporal shore, the Star Maker awakening beneath a sensuous film of water and biologically textured clay.

You are a single field of awareness containing multitudes of constituent beings, each of whom individualizes certain of your qualities, aspects, and interests.

You are each of these spirit beings.

You are one of these spirit beings.

And you are the field that contains them all.

You rise in these material robes to introduce a second movement of the dimensional symphony.

You arrive, surface, awaken in a species of cooperating life forms. A biological family becomes aware of you.

You are welcome behind these eyes, welcome in these warm-blooded temples, these windows, these porthole probes to explore terrestrial shores, ocean floors, and the galaxies that fill your soul.

You are with them now, within them, living, breathing. Through human eyes you see a world of frozen music/matter warming in slow biological combustion, a world where dreams take form, have formed, where vision lives are lived in song, where sensuous enchantment congeals conscious wishes in graceful, organic fields. Where geometric lives appear in shimmering waves of love's eternal heat, and rhythmic energies reveal patterns in the charged creative air. Melodies become beings, creatures here, in these fields . . .

You are moving now, moving within, lifting this cooler ocean-landed world.

Awareness rises like tides of the seas. You are the current within, within the living melodies, the attention beneath these endlessly undulating tapestries whose mysteries ripple outward now, rise upward now, on waves, symphonic waves, the currents of your eternal whole. A panorama of magical, mathematical, musical dimension unfolds, in graceful, shimmering flows. Information, novalike, explodes.

There are tongues in these trees, angels in these libraries . . . healing hands to knead the bread of centuries, and mouths of parted lips to breathe warm genes into all these things.

So you see letters leaving fragrance on these leaves, these leaves you asked to see. They lived once, you know, budding, turning, pages—once-forested terrain—and will live again. For a blue-white water world's refrain crumbles history's walls and lunar echoes sing, "Awareness, awareness, awareness in these worldfalls."

Ocean light years pupils deep, opening now, throwing off the tides of sleep. Eyes of fire in fertile, garden-rich terrain—conscious solar flames . . . streaming starbows' stellar rains . . . cascading, tumbling . . . glowing colors falling, freely flowing . . . swirling round and white-hole-vortex round,

spilling deep . . . into these fields . . .

eternal fields . . .

fields of stars . . .